OPPOSING
VIEWPOINTS®
SERIES

The Environment

Other Books of Related Interest:

Opposing Viewpoints Series

Eco-Architecture

Endangered Oceans

Garbage and Recycling

At Issue Series

Greenhouse Gases

What is the Impact of E-Waste?

Will the World Run Out of Fresh Water?

Current Controversies Series

Global Warming

Pollution

"Congress shall make no law . . . abridging the freedom of speech, or of the press."

First Amendment to the U.S. Constitution

The basic foundation of our democracy is the First Amendment guarantee of freedom of expression. The Opposing Viewpoints Series is dedicated to the concept of this basic freedom and the idea that it is more important to practice it than to enshrine it.

OPPOSING
VIEWPOINTS®
SERIES

The Environment

Louise I. Gerdes, Book Editor

GREENHAVEN PRESS
A part of Gale, Cengage Learning

GALE
CENGAGE Learning™

Detroit • New York • San Francisco • New Haven, Conn • Waterville, Maine • London

GALE
CENGAGE Learning™

Christine Nasso, *Publisher*
Elizabeth Des Chenes, *Managing Editor*

For more information, contact:
Greenhaven Press
27500 Drake Rd.
Farmington Hills, MI 48331-3535
Or you can visit our Internet site at gale.cengage.com

For product information and technology assistance, contact us at

Gale Customer Support, 1-800-877-4253
For permission to use material from this text or product, submit all requests online at www.cengage.com/permissions

Further permissions questions can be emailed to permissionrequest@cengage.com

Articles in Greenhaven Press anthologies are often edited for length to meet page requirements. In addition, original titles of these works are changed to clearly present the main thesis and to explicitly indicate the author's opinion. Every effort is made to ensure that Greenhaven Press accurately reflects the original intent of the authors. Every effort has been made to trace the owners of copyrighted material.

Cover Image Source/Getty Images.

LIBRARY OF CONGRESS CATALOGING-IN-PUBLICATION DATA

The environment / Louise I. Gerdes, book editor.
    p. cm. -- (Opposing viewpoints)
    Includes bibliographical references and index.
    ISBN-13: 978-0-7377-4362-3 (hardcover)
    ISBN-13: 978-0-7377-4361-6 (pbk.)
    1. Environmental sciences. I. Gerdes, Louise I., 1953-
    GE105.E5 2009
    363.7--dc22

                                                                2008055846

Printed in the United States of America
1 2 3 4 5 6 7 13 12 11 10 09

Contents

Chapter 3: Is the Western Lifestyle Bad for the Environment?

Chapter 4: What Policies Will Improve the Environment?

Why Consider Opposing Viewpoints?

> *"The only way in which a human being can make some approach to knowing the whole of a subject is by hearing what can be said about it by persons of every variety of opinion and studying all modes in which it can be looked at by every character of mind. No wise man ever acquired his wisdom in any mode but this."*
>
> *John Stuart Mill*

In our media-intensive culture it is not difficult to find differing opinions. Thousands of newspapers and magazines and dozens of radio and television talk shows resound with differing points of view. The difficulty lies in deciding which opinion to agree with and which "experts" seem the most credible. The more inundated we become with differing opinions and claims, the more essential it is to hone critical reading and thinking skills to evaluate these ideas. Opposing Viewpoints books address this problem directly by presenting stimulating debates that can be used to enhance and teach these skills. The varied opinions contained in each book examine many different aspects of a single issue. While examining these conveniently edited opposing views, readers can develop critical thinking skills such as the ability to compare and contrast authors' credibility, facts, argumentation styles, use of persuasive techniques, and other stylistic tools. In short, the Opposing Viewpoints Series is an ideal way to attain the higher-level thinking and reading skills so essential in a culture of diverse and contradictory opinions.

In addition to providing a tool for critical thinking, Opposing Viewpoints books challenge readers to question their own strongly held opinions and assumptions. Most people form their opinions on the basis of upbringing, peer pressure, and personal, cultural, or professional bias. By reading carefully balanced opposing views, readers must directly confront new ideas as well as the opinions of those with whom they disagree. This is not to simplistically argue that everyone who reads opposing views will—or should—change his or her opinion. Instead, the series enhances readers' understanding of their own views by encouraging confrontation with opposing ideas. Careful examination of others' views can lead to the readers' understanding of the logical inconsistencies in their own opinions, perspective on why they hold an opinion, and the consideration of the possibility that their opinion requires further evaluation.

Evaluating Other Opinions

To ensure that this type of examination occurs, Opposing Viewpoints books present all types of opinions. Prominent spokespeople on different sides of each issue as well as well-known professionals from many disciplines challenge the reader. An additional goal of the series is to provide a forum for other, less known, or even unpopular viewpoints. The opinion of an ordinary person who has had to make the decision to cut off life support from a terminally ill relative, for example, may be just as valuable and provide just as much insight as a medical ethicist's professional opinion. The editors have two additional purposes in including these less known views. One, the editors encourage readers to respect others' opinions—even when not enhanced by professional credibility. It is only by reading or listening to and objectively evaluating others' ideas that one can determine whether they are worthy of consideration. Two, the inclusion of such viewpoints encourages the important critical thinking skill of objectively evaluating an author's credentials and bias. This evaluation will illuminate an author's reasons for taking a particular stance on an issue and will aid in readers' evaluation of the author's ideas.

It is our hope that these books will give readers a deeper understanding of the issues debated and an appreciation of the complexity of even seemingly simple issues when good and honest people disagree. This awareness is particularly important in a democratic society such as ours in which people enter into public debate to determine the common good. Those with whom one disagrees should not be regarded as enemies but rather as people whose views deserve careful examination and may shed light on one's own.

Thomas Jefferson once said that "difference of opinion leads to inquiry, and inquiry to truth." Jefferson, a broadly educated man, argued that "if a nation expects to be ignorant and free . . . it expects what never was and never will be." As individuals and as a nation, it is imperative that we consider the opinions of others and examine them with skill and discernment. The Opposing Viewpoints Series is intended to help readers achieve this goal.

David L. Bender and Bruno Leone,
Founders

Introduction

> "The environmental movement in America is complex and multifaceted. It includes national, regional, and local organizations. The movement has spiritual, religious, scientific, and secular dimensions."
>
> —Bill Devall,
> conservation activist and professor,
> Humboldt State University,
> Arcata, California.

From the beginning, America's relationship with the environment has been fraught with tension. On the one hand, the American wilderness has been a source of great national pride. In fact, a frontier spirit is considered by many to be part of America's national identity. Early twentieth century historian Frederick Jackson Turner, author of *The Significance of the Frontier in American History*, proclaimed that the American character "came out of the forests and gained new strength each time it touched a frontier." On the other hand, the American wilderness also has been a source of national prosperity, its vast resources to be conquered and exploited. The tension between these two often conflicting attitudes toward America's natural resources continues to this day. Indeed, the historical friction between those who want to protect and conserve the environment and the social forces that often place significant stress on the natural world is the crux of the environmental debate today.

During the late nineteenth and early twentieth century, the desire to preserve and conserve the American wilderness was strong. Inspired by essays and poems written by such distinguished writers as Henry David Thoreau and James Russell

Lowell, Congress began to recognize the scenic and recreational value of a pristine environment. In 1871 Congress established Yellowstone as the world's first national park. By the end of the first decade of the twentieth century, President Theodore Roosevelt had inspired Congress to double the acreage devoted to national parks and wildlife sanctuaries. Congress also passed legislation to protect fur-bearing animals in Alaska, fisheries in the Atlantic, and forests on government lands. The first environmental organization, the Sierra Club, was founded by writer John Muir and some of his friends in 1892. Muir's eloquent works, which expressed the spiritual value of nature, were published in influential magazines, and the American passion for protecting wilderness areas grew. However, those environmentalists who followed Muir would soon experience the tension between competing interests in America's natural resources.

During the prosperous, "roaring" twenties, the environmental pendulum swung toward exploitation. According to activist and sociology professor Bill Devall, during this period "the social forces of urbanization, industrial growth, expansion of trade, and accelerating population growth were more powerful in America than the recreational, scenic, and spiritual values that Muir espoused." Reflective of the power of these social forces was the failure of Muir and the Sierra Club to block the construction of a dam and reservoir on the Tuolumne River in Hetch Hetchy Valley in Yosemite National Park. Many favored the dam because it would provide water for the growing population of San Francisco, which had recently suffered a devastating earthquake and fire in 1906. The O'Shaughnessy Dam was completed in 1923, and San Francisco began using the Hetch Hetchy Reservoir for its water supply and electricity shortly thereafter. In addition to authorizing hydroelectric projects that dredged and dammed inland waters, during the early twentieth century, Congress made federal lands available to mining and drilling for a nominal fee. On the American plains, agricultural practices designed to maximize production at the expense of the land contributed to the massive dust storms that turned the nation's bountiful farmland into the Dust Bowl.

The prosperity of the twenties did not last, and the United States plunged into an economic depression. During the years during and following the Great Depression, valued groups such as the Sierra Club would continue to defend valued spaces—the Sierra Nevada, the shores of Lake Michigan, the Florida Everglades, and the desert southwest. Nevertheless, efforts to combat the depression and later to fight World War II put social forces before environmental concerns. Following the war, however, a new environmental movement was born. While the early environmental movement was inspired by the words of John Muir, many historians claim that Rachel Carson's 1962 book *Silent Spring* foreshadowed the forthcoming era of environmental activism. The book induced national outrage against agriculture practices employed at the expense of wild nature. Carson exposed the hazards of the pesticide DDT and eloquently challenged humanity's faith in technological progress. After decades of rapid population growth, industrial expansion, and suburban sprawl following World War II, American attitudes had once again shifted toward protecting, rather than exploiting, America's natural resources.

Indeed, many consider the 1970s the era of environmental activism. According to then Senator Gaylord Nelson, the first Earth Day, on April 22, 1970, was a way to "shake up the political establishment and force this issue onto the national agenda." Policymakers appeared to get the message. Not only did President Richard M. Nixon establish the Environmental Protection Agency, but Congress passed the Clean Air Act, the Clean Water Act, the Endangered Species Act, the Marine Mammal Protection Act, the Safe Drinking Water Act, the Toxic Substances Control Act, and the Resource Conservation and Recovery Act. It also banned DDT and phased out leaded gasoline and ozone-destroying chlorofluorocarbons. In fact, the environmental movement was so strong that it gave birth to Green political parties.

Environmental legislation slowed, however, in the 1980s, during what some call a period of environmental backlash. Although Congress established the Superfund program, which began to clean up hazardous waste sites during this decade, the administration of President Ronald Reagan saw a significant erosion of environmental laws. To counter the backlash, the environmental movement began to pursue what they called the "third way," appealing directly to specific corporations to change their practices—a strategy that many environmental organizations continue to use today. Environmentalists, suggests Sierra Club representative Eric Antebi, "can't wait for the federal government, which is why you're seeing all these other players take the first steps."

The primary environmental issue of the 1990s that has continued into the new millennium is the threat posed by global warming. In fact, the tension between the American desire to protect the environment and the conflicting desire to prosper using the nation's natural resources is probably best reflected in the climate-change controversy. While a majority of Americans believe that addressing global warming should be a top priority, the United States has yet to ratify the Kyoto Protocol, which calls for mandatory reductions in the greenhouse gases that many scientists claim have caused global warming. Critics claim that efforts to meet the stringent demands of the Protocol would threaten the U.S. economy—once again reflecting the tension between protecting the environment and promoting prosperity.

The inherent conflict among views—that environmental policies should promote conservation and protection of the environment and, alternatively, that environmental policies should not interfere with the American pursuit of prosperity—remains one of the fundamental controversies in the environmental debate. This tension is, in fact, reflected in many of the viewpoints presented in the following chapters of *Opposing Viewpoints: The Environment*: Is There an Environmental Crisis? How Should Global Warming Be Addressed? Is the Western Lifestyle Bad for the Environment? and What Policies Will Improve the Environment? Former U.S. Secretary of the Interior Stewart Udall believed that resolving the tension between preserving or exploiting the nation's resources would require a new attitude. In *The Quiet Crisis*, Udall argues that "only an ever-widening concept and higher ideal of conservation will enlist our finest impulses and move us to make the earth a better home both for ourselves and for those as yet unborn." Whether policymakers will heed these words remains to be seen.

OPPOSING
VIEWPOINTS®
SERIES

CHAPTER 1

Is There an Environmental Crisis?

Chapter Preface

The number of animals in large-scale livestock-production systems, also known as factory farms, has increased significantly since 1982. The amount of waste produced by these farms has in turn increased. According to a September 2008 U.S. Government Accountability Office report, a farm with 800,000 hogs or 140,000 head of cattle could produce more than 1.6 million tons of manure per year, which is one and one-half times more than the sanitary waste produced each year by the city of Philadelphia. The gases released from such animal farms are a major source of greenhouse gases. Indeed, a 2006 United Nations report concluded that the meat industry causes almost 50 percent more greenhouse gas emissions than all the world's cars, trucks, sport utility vehicles, planes, and ships. Unfortunately, natural processes cannot neutralize this factory-farming waste. As a result, some commentators claim, the intense concentration of waste degrades the land, water, and air quality and makes factory-farm workers and neighbors ill. In response, activists have increased pressure to regulate factory-farm waste in the same way other industry pollutants are regulated. However, under pressure from those who represent factory farmers, the U.S. Environmental Protection Agency (EPA) has proposed exempting factory farms from the reporting requirements already in place. This debate over factory-farm waste is one of several controversies in the environmental debate.

Meat industry representatives, however, deny claims that factory farms pose a threat to the environment or to human health and therefore oppose strict regulation. In fact, many industry analysts assert that animal waste should not be listed as a pollutant. More than 130 representatives from agricultural states sponsored a bill that would remove animal waste from the list of toxic environmental pollutants under the Superfund statute, the federal environmental clean-up law. Factory farmers in many agricultural states have been threatened by lawsuits that charge factory farms with polluting water sources. "Congress never intended for Superfund to apply to farms, but the judicial system has done just that, threatening the livelihood of farmers and ranchers everywhere," claims U.S. Representative Collin C. Peterson (D-Minnesota). Those who oppose the strict regulation of factory farms also argue that regulation and the cost of defending lawsuits will drive up the price of food.

On the other hand, commentators who claim that strict regulation of factory farms is necessary say such increases in food costs would be minimal. In their view, any increases would not be significant enough to remove reporting regulations that are often the only tool communities have to hold factory farms accountable for the pollution they produce. "We're talking pennies," claims John Carlin of Kansas State University. "When you factor in the positives from the standpoint of public health and the environment, it would actually save us money," Carlin contends. Still others fear that erosion of laws that regulate the pollution from these operations will threaten state and local efforts that impose tougher regulations than does the federal government. "State and local regulators are steamed because [relaxing EPA rules is] going to undermine their ability to regulate these air pollution emissions, these health threats," argues William Becker, executive director of the States and Territorial Air Pollution Program Administrators.

Whether factory-farm waste is a serious environmental threat that should be strictly regulated remains hotly contested. The authors in the following chapter debate other issues in answer to the question, is there is an environmental crisis?

> "Nothing can prevent large parts of the
> planet becoming too hot to inhabit, or
> sinking underwater, resulting in mass
> migration, famine and epidemics."

The Earth Faces an Environmental Crisis

Decca Aitkenhead

According to British scientist James Lovelock, an environmental crisis is inevitable because global warming is irreversible, reports British journalist Decca Aitkenhead in the following viewpoint. In the 1960s Lovelock introduced the controversial Gaia hypothesis, the theory, now generally accepted, that the Earth is a self-regulating organism. He now contends that significant parts of the Earth will soon be too hot to inhabit and others will sink underwater. As a result, he claims, the world will face mass migration, famine, and widespread epidemics. Unfortunately, most solutions such as renewable energy will be inadequate to save humanity, Lovelock maintains.

Decca Aitkenhead, "Enjoy Life While You Can," *The Guardian*, March 1, 2008, p. 33. Copyright © 2008 Guardian Newspapers Limited. Reproduced by permission of Guardian News Service, LTD.

As you read, consider the following questions:

1. How does Lovelock respond to those who say that he should not make claims about the severity and the irreversibility of the environmental catastrophe?

2. What does Lovelock believe is humanity's only chance of survival?

3. In Lovelock's opinion, how much of the world's population will be wiped out by 2100?

In 1965 executives at Shell wanted to know what the world would look like in the year 2000. They consulted a range of experts, who speculated about fusion-powered hovercrafts and "all sorts of fanciful technological stuff". When the oil company asked the scientist James Lovelock, he predicted that the main problem in 2000 would be the environment. "It will be worsening then to such an extent that it will seriously affect their business," he said.

"And of course," Lovelock says, with a smile 43 years later, "that's almost exactly what's happened."

A Pattern of Accurate Predictions

Lovelock has been dispensing predictions from his one-man laboratory in an old mill in Cornwall [Great Britain] since the mid-1960s, the consistent accuracy of which have earned him a reputation as one of Britain's most respected—if maverick—independent scientists. Working alone since the age of 40, he invented a device that detected CFCs [chlorofluorocarbons], which helped detect the growing hole in the ozone layer, and introduced the Gaia hypothesis, a revolutionary theory that the Earth is a self-regulating super-organism. Initially ridiculed by many scientists as new age nonsense, today that theory forms the basis of almost all climate science.

For decades, his advocacy of nuclear power appalled fellow environmentalists—but recently increasing numbers of them have come around to his way of thinking. His latest book, *The*

Revenge of Gaia, predicts that by 2020 extreme weather will be the norm, causing global devastation; that by 2040 much of Europe will be Saharan; and parts of London will be underwater. The most recent Intergovernmental Panel on Climate Change (IPCC) report deploys less dramatic language—but its calculations aren't a million miles away from his.

As with most people, my panic about climate change is equalled only by my confusion over what I ought to do about it. A meeting with Lovelock therefore feels a little like an audience with a prophet. Buried down a winding track through wild woodland, in an office full of books and papers and contraptions involving dials and wires, the 88-year-old presents his thoughts with a quiet, unshakable conviction that can be unnerving. More alarming even than his apocalyptic climate predictions is his utter certainty that almost everything we're trying to do about it is wrong.

On the day we meet, [the British newspaper] the *Daily Mail* has launched a campaign to rid Britain of plastic shopping bags. The initiative sits comfortably within the current canon of eco ideas, next to ethical consumption, carbon offsetting, recycling and so on—all of which are premised on the calculation that individual lifestyle adjustments can still save the planet. This is, Lovelock says, a deluded fantasy. Most of the things we have been told to do might make us feel better, but they won't make any difference. Global warming has passed the tipping point, and catastrophe is unstoppable.

Lovelock Responds to Fears and Misconceptions

"It's just too late for it," he says. "Perhaps if we'd gone along routes like that in 1967, it might have helped. But we don't have time. All these standard green things, like sustainable development, I think these are just words that mean nothing. I get an awful lot of people coming to me saying you can't say that, because it gives us nothing to do. I say on the contrary, it gives us an immense amount to do. Just not the kinds of things you want to do."

He dismisses eco ideas briskly, one by one. "Carbon offsetting? I wouldn't dream of it. It's just a joke to pay money to plant trees, to think you're offsetting the carbon? You're probably making matters worse. You're far better off giving to the charity Cool Earth, which gives the money to the native peoples to not take down their forests."

Do he and his wife try to limit the number of flights they take? "No we don't. Because we can't." And recycling, he adds, is "almost certainly a waste of time and energy", while having a "green lifestyle" amounts to little more than "ostentatious grand gestures". He distrusts the notion of ethical consumption. "Because always, in the end, it turns out to be a scam . . . or if it wasn't one in the beginning, it becomes one."

Somewhat unexpectedly, Lovelock concedes that the *Mail*'s plastic bag campaign seems, "on the face of it, a good thing". But it transpires that this is largely a tactical response; he regards it as merely more rearrangement of Titanic deckchairs, "but I've learnt there's no point in causing a quarrel over everything". He saves his thunder for what he considers the emptiest false promise of all—renewable energy.

"You're never going to get enough energy from wind to run a society such as ours," he says. "Windmills! Oh no. No way of doing it. You can cover the whole country with the blasted things, millions of them. Waste of time."

This is all delivered with an air of benign wonder at the intractable stupidity of people. "I see it with everybody. People just want to go on doing what they're doing. They want business as usual. They say, 'Oh yes, there's going to be a problem up ahead,' but they don't want to change anything."

An Irreversible Problem

Lovelock believes global warming is now irreversible, and that nothing can prevent large parts of the planet becoming too

An Unpredictable Environment

The bad news is that mankind has so profoundly transformed the earth that nature's ability to produce the goods and services that are essential for human life (fertile soils protected against erosion; potable water; clean air; a diversity of genetic resources permitting the development of pharmaceutical and agricultural products; ample supplies of fish, game, and fuel; protection against flood; climatic stability; the natural beauty that nourishes the spiritual, aesthetic, and symbolic life of human societies; and so on) is gravely threatened—to the point that the response of the natural environment to further escalation of human pressures upon it has become unpredictable. . . .

The good news is that mankind has given proof throughout its history of a great capacity to adapt to changes in its environment.

Eric Lambin, The Middle Path: Avoiding Environmental Catastrophe, *University of Chicago Press, 2007.*

hot to inhabit, or sinking underwater, resulting in mass migration, famine and epidemics. Britain is going to become a lifeboat for refugees from mainland Europe, so instead of wasting our time on wind turbines we need to start planning how to survive. To Lovelock, the logic is clear. The sustainability brigade are insane to think we can save ourselves by going back to nature; our only chance of survival will come not from less technology, but more.

Nuclear power, he argues, can solve our energy problem—the bigger challenge will be food. "Maybe they'll synthesise food. I don't know. Synthesising food is not some mad visionary idea; you can buy it in Tesco's, in the form of Quorn. It's not that good, but people buy it. You can live on it." But he fears we won't invent the necessary technologies in time, and expects "about 80%" of the world's population to be wiped out by 2100. Prophets have been foretelling Armageddon since time began, he says. "But this is the real thing."

Faced with two versions of the future—Kyoto's preventative action and Lovelock's apocalypse—who are we to believe? Some critics have suggested Lovelock's readiness to concede the fight against climate change owes more to old age than science: "People who say that about me haven't reached my age," he says laughing.

But when I ask if he attributes the conflicting predictions to differences in scientific understanding or personality, he says: "Personality."

A Fondness for Heresy?

There's more than a hint of the controversialist in his work, and it seems an unlikely coincidence that Lovelock became convinced of the irreversibility of climate change in 2004, at the very point when the international consensus was coming round to the need for urgent action. Aren't his theories at least partly driven by a fondness for heresy?

"Not a bit! Not a bit! All I want is a quiet life! But I can't help noticing when things happen, when you go out and find something. People don't like it because it upsets their ideas."

But the suspicion seems confirmed when I ask if he's found it rewarding to see many of his climate change warnings endorsed by the IPCC. "Oh no! In fact, I'm writing another book now, I'm about a third of the way into it, to try and take the next steps ahead."

Interviewers often remark upon the discrepancy between Lovelock's predictions of doom, and his good humour. "Well I'm cheerful!" he says, smiling. "I'm an optimist. It's going to happen."

Humanity is in a period exactly like 1938–9, he explains, when "we all knew something terrible was going to happen, but didn't know what to do about it". But once the second world war was under way "everyone got excited, they loved the things they could do, it was one long holiday . . . so when I think of the impending crisis now, I think in those terms. A sense of purpose—that's what people want."

At moments I wonder about Lovelock's credentials as a prophet. Sometimes he seems less clear-eyed with scientific vision than disposed to see the version of the future his prejudices are looking for. A socialist as a young man, he now favours market forces, and it's not clear whether his politics are the child or the father of his science. His hostility to renewable energy, for example, gets expressed in strikingly Eurosceptic terms of irritation with subsidies and bureaucrats. But then, when he talks about the Earth—or Gaia—it is in the purest scientific terms all.

"There have been seven disasters since humans came on the earth, very similar to the one that's just about to happen. I think these events keep separating the wheat from the chaff. And eventually we'll have a human on the planet that really does understand it and can live with it properly. That's the source of my optimism."

What would Lovelock do now, I ask, if he were me? He smiles and says: "Enjoy life while you can. Because if you're lucky it's going to be 20 years before it hits the fan."

| "Might some of the most extreme efforts at reduction [of greenhouse gas emissions] create a crisis of a different kind?"

Environmental Alarmism Poses a Serious Threat

Jon Entine

Environmental alarmism leads to ridiculous and irresponsible conservation efforts that could radically set back the U.S. standard of living, argues Jon Entine in the following viewpoint. Efforts to cut greenhouse gas emissions 80 percent by 2050 would require turning back emissions to those produced in 1875, he claims. The U.S. gross domestic product could drop as much as 10.1 percent, Entine contends. Efforts to meet these unrealistic targets based on uncertain predictions is absurd, he reasons. Entine is a fellow at American Enterprise Institute, a libertarian think tank.

As you read, consider the following questions:

1. According to Entine, what would it cost to reduce greenhouse gas emissions in the United States during the next 20 years?

Jon Entine, "How Green Hysteria Will Hit Home," *Ethical Corporation*, May 6, 2008. Copyright © 2008 *Ethical Corporation*. Reproduced by permission.

2. What evidence proves that American greenhouse gas emissions are in line with those of most European nations, in the author's view?

3. In the author's opinion, by what percentage would carbon dioxide (CO_2) emissions exceed the 2050 target even if every car matched the emissions performance of a Toyota Prius?

Let's call it the black box syndrome: making revolutionary changes or new products without any real handle on what has actually been created or the potential impact. No-one really knew what the risks were when the wizards of Wall Street launched the inscrutable credit products that led to the current financial bubble that is now imploding, rocking the world economy.

The Rhetoric of Catastrophe

Now we have something akin to that bubble building in the environmental arena, in the inflated rhetoric on global warming rising inexorably from the environmental-political complex. Global warming is a fact. The great questions are not whether the environment is gradually warming but whether it will persist and if so what can or should be done about it— and at what costs.

Alarmists-by-anecdote invoke Katrina [hurricane in August 2005], melting ice caps and death-by-heatstroke as signs of the end of the world as we know it. "It has been harder and harder to misinterpret the signs that our world is spinning out of kilter," Al Gore said [in 2007] in his acceptance speech for the Nobel Peace Prize.

But the inconvenient truth is that we have just emerged from two of the calmest storm seasons on record and one of the coldest winters in decades. Of course, one year or even ten does not constitute a long-term trend, which is why the [2007] report by the Intergovernmental Panel on Climate

Change [IPCC] deploys the words "uncertain" or "uncertainty" more than 1,300 times in 900 pages.

Uncertainty aside, politics offers up the rhetoric of catastrophe and solutions. With the cognoscenti [experts] lambasting the US as the world's leading miscreant in the global warming arena, [2008] Republican presidential candidate John McCain says he would reduce greenhouse gas emissions by 65 per cent by 2050, while the two Democrat contenders, Barack Obama and Hillary Clinton, embrace 80 per cent, in line with the demands of European activists.

Here's the environmental black box: considering the uncertainties voiced by the IPCC, should we embark on an immediate, drastic, and massively expensive reduction in greenhouse gas emissions? Are such goals even achievable, or might some of the most extreme efforts at reduction create a crisis of a different kind?

To address these thorny issues, let us focus on the US. One recent projection from the liberal Clean Fuels Institute at City University in New York estimates it would cost, conservatively, $6 trillion over the next 20 years to flatten greenhouse gases emissions in the US and tens of trillions more to meet the "progressive" targets over 40 years.

Compare those costs against the worst-case scenario of the credit meltdown. That might cost the financial system $1 trillion, according to the International Monetary Fund—enough to raise legitimate worries about a worldwide depression. But those potential losses are only the tiniest fraction of the economic repercussions that would result from actually meeting the expected 2050 global warming targets.

Crunching the Numbers and Assessing the Targets

Steven Hayward, a resident fellow at the American Enterprise Institute in Washington DC, and an expert on environmental economics, is one of the few people who have actually

Environmental Alarmism Is Anti-Human

Industry runs on energy, but you cannot directly attack the energy source because this would alienate the vast majority of the public who benefit from industrialization. The easiest way is to show that the byproducts of industrial activity are causing a planetary collapse. . . .

There are negative side-effects of industrialization of course, but eliminating industry also eliminates its exceptionally beneficial impacts on quality of life. Besides ignoring the natural evolution of the human species, in the extreme, today's climate alarmism is decidedly anti-human. Human progress is seen, not as a natural evolution, but an unnatural aberration.

Tim Ball & Tom Harris, "Climate Extremism: The Real Threat to Civilization," Canada Free Press, *July 20, 2007.*

crunched the numbers. In his [2008] "Index of Leading Environmental Indicators", Hayward raises some "inconvenient truths", as he likes to say, including putting in context the knee-jerk European belief that the US is a slacker in reducing greenhouse gas emissions [GHGs]. The US starts from a higher base because of the longer transportation distances and larger homes (twice the size of the average European dwelling), but when these differences are normalised, American GHG emissions are in line with those of most European nations.

Because of accelerating conservation efforts, the US was the only industrialised country in which greenhouse gas emissions fell during the most recent year data is available, 2006. The 1.5 per cent reduction marked the first time emissions have ever fallen in a non-recessionary year. It also has the best record of restraining greenhouse gas emissions over the past eight years. While Kyoto-protocol participants increased 21.1 per cent, US emissions increased only 6.6 per cent.

But the most provocative part of Hayward's report is when he takes the abstract costs to reduce GHG emissions and translates them into real life. How would Mom and Pop be affected if the "progressives" achieve their goal of an 80 per cent reduction? As Hayward notes, on average each person in the US generates almost 20 tonnes of CO_2 [carbon dioxide] from fossil fuel usage. To give some idea of how radical an 80 per cent reduction would be, consider that Botswana, Haiti, and Somalia operate at that level today. It would entail turning back the per capita emissions output to 1875, when wood burning was a primary heat source.

What would such a reduction mean to the average homeowner? Each American home today produces over 11 tonnes of emissions per year. To meet the 2050 target Hayward figures each household could emit 1.5 tonnes of CO_2. That's more than the average family emits using just one appliance—their hot water heater. Forget such "luxuries" as a refrigerator, freezer, washer and dryer, let alone a flat-screen TV.

The transportation sector would get creamed. That SUV or visiting the relatives in California? Forget it. Today's consumption of jet fuel alone accounts for two-thirds of the 2050 target. Hayward notes that the last time the transportation infrastructure operated at the target consumption level was during the 1920s, when commercial air travel was negligible and there were 26 million cars and trucks—compared with more than 246 million today. Hayward says: "If the entire auto industry today matched the performance of today's Toyota Prius, CO_2 emissions would be . . . 40 per cent higher than the 2050 emissions target."

A Drop in Gross Domestic Product

What would be the overall impact on the economy of meeting the radical reduction targets? In March [2008], the US Environmental Protection Agency released its analysis of the proposed Lieberman-Warner Environmental Security Act, which is designed to reduce emissions by 70 per cent by 2050. It projects that GDP [Gross Domestic Product] could drop 2.7 per cent, which would be far worse than the current financial crisis, but that's at a minimum. It projected GDP could very well fall a catastrophic 10.1 per cent—setting back the standard of living in the US and the world by decades.

The respected strategists Robert Socolow and Stephen Pacala of Princeton University, in their well-received report on seven aggressive "stabilisation wedge" energy strategies, argued that it would take enormous, and politically unacceptable, sacrifices to just hold CO_2 emissions steady. In short, the 2050 targets are both absurd and irresponsible.

Without radical breakthroughs in geo-engineering through, say, injecting high altitude sulphate particles in the atmosphere, we are going to have to focus our limited economic resources on adaptation. That could mean everything from trying to develop GM [genetically modified] crops that use less water to designing waterfront systems that protect against rising waters, structures pioneered years ago by the Dutch, rather than setting pie-in-the-sky GHG reduction targets.

"It's crying wolf," says Hayward on the projections of catastrophic climate change and the calls for a dramatic overhaul of society to address these projections. "Even if they are right, they are squandering their moral authority. If you're looking for technological solutions instead of exaggeration, sadly you won't find it in most discussions about climate change."

Let's hope the air continues to leak out of the climate change hysteria bubble, and the quicker the better.

> "Scientists now are highly confident—
> more than 90 percent certain—that the
> [climate] change we have seen is real
> anthropogenic, here to stay, and grow-
> ing worse."

Global Warming
Is a Serious Problem

William Chandler

Most scientists agree that global warming is a serious problem with human causes, maintains William Chandler in the following viewpoint. In the coming centuries, he asserts, temperatures will get warmer and seas will rise due to the release of greenhouse gases. Despite growing acceptance of the existence of the problem, however, efforts to reduce greenhouse gases have been limited, Chandler claims. To respond effectively, he argues, nations worldwide must stop shifting blame and work together to develop efficient alternative energy sources. Chandler is president of Transition Energy and co-founder of DEED China, and both companies have energy efficiency projects in China.

William Chandler, "Our First Response to Climate Change," *World Watch*, November/December 2007, pp. 10–11. Copyright © 2007 WorldWatch Institute. Reproduced by permission.

As you read, consider the following questions:

1. What climate changes does Chandler cite as evidence of global warming?

2. What does the author contend are some of the few positive signs of policy change?

3. According to the author, why is encouraging markets to implement efficiency a difficult task?

"Time is passing very quickly," Irving Mintzer wrote in his 1987 study *A Matter of Degrees*, which I reviewed for the very first edition of *World Watch*. Two decades later, Mintzer's words, like his report on ways to reduce the risk of global warming, seem understated.

It was later than it seemed. Even those of us who have long been alarmed about global warming did not expect the rapid changes we have seen.

We have watched the northern polar ice cap melt over an area the size of Alaska. We have seen glaciers shrink on every continent while the depth of snow in the Swiss Alps fell by half. We have experienced twice as many hurricanes per year as our parents, and measured them growing stronger year by year. We might have known, when *World Watch* was launched, that New Orleans was vulnerable to flood, but we have all been shocked by the devastating force of Hurricane Katrina.

A Scientific Consensus

Scientists now are highly confident—more than 90 percent certain—that the change we have seen is real anthropogenic, here to stay, and growing worse. We know this because, since it was founded in 1988, there have been four sweeping assessments of climate science, impacts, and emissions mitigation by the Intergovernmental Panel on Climate Change (IPCC). The IPCC [in 2007] published its Fourth Assessment Report and the scientists' concern was palpable.

Their consensus view is that warmer days and nights are virtually certain in the coming century, or centuries, and that the cause is the release of greenhouse gases mainly from energy use. Sea levels may rise by meters rather than the meter we expected. The worst impacts will be suffered by the poor, especially those living in low-lying agricultural lands like Bangladesh. As climate scientist Stephen Schneider of Stanford University put it recently in the *New York Times*, "You don't want to be poor and living on a river delta or the Florida coast."

Policy change, meanwhile, has been glacial (in the now obsolete sense of the word). Positive signs are few. Europe has implemented the Kyoto Protocol, putting into practice important mechanisms to spur emissions reductions at home and to finance them in developing countries. China has announced ambitious plans to cut energy waste in industry and improve automobile fuel economy. The Soviet Union collapsed a few years after the launch of this magazine, ending the world's most egregious forms of energy waste. Even some in the United States seem to be taking action, with almost 20 states having announced plans and policies to cut greenhouse gas emissions.

But these examples are not proportionate to the challenge. Imagine if this were war and we so meekly surrendered our coastal cities.

The worst scenarios of warming described in Mintzer's 20-year-old paper may yet be realized. Mintzer in a recent conversation said that he thinks we have at most 10 years to mount a serious response that will avoid catastrophic change. If that is true—and I believe it is—then there is no time to develop a magic bullet. Technology, unless it is ready to be deployed now, will not save the natural world as we know it.

A response appropriate to reality will require climbing above the reflexive nationalism, racism, and fears that shape our international affairs. It is fashionable to point to China

The Estimated Global Warming Price Tag				
	In billions of dollars			
	2025	**2050**	**2075**	**2100**
◇ Hurricane Damages	$10	$43	$142	$422
⌂ Real Estate Losses	$34	$80	$173	$360
◈ Energy-Sector Costs	$28	$47	$82	$141
◊ Water Costs	$200	$336	$565	$950
Total	**$271**	**$506**	**$961**	**$1,873**

Note: Totals may not add up exactly due to rounding.

TAKEN FROM: Fred Ackerman and Elizabeth A. Stanton, National Resources Defense Council, in "The Cost of Climate Change: What We'll Pay if Global Warming Continues Unchecked," May 2008.

and India, their rapid energy demand growth and increasing wealth, and to demand that they take responsibility for their actions.

It is not that simple. China already suffers from air and water pollution crises that kill tens of thousands of its citizens each year. India is unable to supply adequate electric power to several hundred million of its people, and they suffer the attendant drudgery and ill health. Who can blame the governments of these and other developing countries for pointing out that the per-capita greenhouse gas emissions of their populations are one-fifth that of Americans and saying, "You created this problem, you do something about it."

A Global Accord

That is not an answer either, of course. A serious response will require the participation of all the world's leading nations. What could move the United States, China, India, Europe, and Japan to work together on a global accord?

One vision is to catalogue all the low-carbon energy alternatives and ask the world's governments to subsidize and compel their use. But market penetration of wind and solar will take decades, nuclear plants contain plutonium and thus the germ of nuclear terror, and scrubbing and sequestering carbon from coal-fired power plants is two decades down the road—outside Mintzer's 10-year time frame.

Maybe we are asking the wrong question. A recent United Nations Foundation team argued that, without energy efficiency, none of the other energy solutions will work. It is, in the words of Thomas Jefferson, the extraordinary—revolutionary—event necessary to enable all the ordinary events to continue.

Maybe the right question is, how can China and the United States work together to build a safe, comfortable, affordable, high-efficiency automobile. Or how can India build efficiency into its power generating systems—and the ways power is used—as the country develops?

Making markets work to implement efficiency is hard. Investors balk not only because of real and perceived risks, but because they do not quite know how to invest in it. Intervention to reduce energy demand requires a lot of work.

A better question is how we can replicate the good sense of the International Finance Corporation which, unlike so many programs, seems to have figured out, in China, Central Europe, and elsewhere, how to rapidly finance and provide technical assistance for energy efficiency investment projects.

Maybe the answers are in learning how to do the small things, rather than in putting together all the world's leaders to talk. Maybe it's time to pay attention to what people do and not what they say.

"'The death of [global warming] theory will be painful and ugly. But it will die. Because it is wrong, wrong, wrong.'"

Global Warming Is Not a Serious Problem

Dennis Behreandt

Despite widespread claims to the contrary, many scientists dispute the assertion that global warming poses a serious global threat, argues Dennis Behreandt in the following viewpoint. Moreover, he asserts, many of these scientists maintain that carbon emissions are not the cause of climate change. According to Behreandt, some scientists suggest that despite substantial increases in carbon dioxide (CO_2) in the decades following World War II, the world in fact began to cool, which is evidence that there is no relation between CO_2 emissions and global warming. Behreandt, a writer and historian, writes frequently for The New American, *a conservative magazine.*

As you read, consider the following questions:

1. What does Behreandt argue is the central idea behind the United Nation's climate alarmism?

Dennis Behreandt, "Global-Warming: Myths Exposed," *New American*, January 7, 2008, pp. 31-32. Copyright © 2008 American Opinion Publishing Incorporated. Reproduced by permission.

2. What evidence does the author give that global warming causes an increase in carbon dioxide?

3. In the author's opinion, how does the Medieval Warm Period support the claim that global warming causes increases in CO_2?

Don't look now, but it's the end of the world. That's the message out of the UN [United Nations] climate meeting in Bali held the week of December 9 [2007]. Bali makes the perfect backdrop for global-warming propaganda—being but six degrees below the equator, it is always warm. In contrast, it wouldn't have done any good for the climate fear mongers to have held their meeting in the Northern Hemisphere, gripped as it is in the middle of winter, especially were it emanating, say, from ice-storm ravaged Des Moines, Iowa.

In sunny Bali, however, the gloves were off with UN Secretary-General Ban Kimoon warning that we are now standing at the point of no return. "The situation is so desperately serious that any delay could push us past the tipping point, beyond which the ecological, financial and human costs would increase dramatically. We are at a crossroads: one path leads to a comprehensive climate change agreement, the other one to oblivion," the UN leader said on December 11. But don't take his word for it, he averred. No doubt thinking about the various reports from the Intergovernmental Panel on Climate Change (IPCC), he claimed: "The world's scientists have spoken with one voice: the situation is grim and urgent action is needed."

The Other Side of the Story

Those who have seen the British documentary *The Great Global Warming Swindle* know for a fact that that last claim is completely untrue. There are, in fact, a large number of very serious and knowledgeable scientists who thoroughly disagree with the UN's notion that climate change is a global catastrophe in the making. Until recently, however, audiences in North America have not had access to the British documentary. It was shown, with great fanfare, on television in the UK [United Kingdom] and Australia, but with the exception of brief appearances of the film on the Internet, American audiences, whose daily lives are otherwise saturated with global-warming scare stories from the Weather Channel, the History Channel, the Discovery Channel, and others, have not been given the other side of the story.

Fortunately, writer and director Martin Durkin's masterpiece is now available on DVD for American audiences. It is a devastating response to the Al Gore-fueled thesis that mankind is destroying the world through carbon emissions. Though it was Gore who was infamously awarded a Nobel Prize for his movie *An Inconvenient Truth*, it is Durkin's *The Great Global Warming Swindle* that is far and away the best documentary film on the subject of global warming, and one which may prove to be the most important documentary film of the last several decades.

The central idea behind the UN's climate alarmism is the idea that man-made carbon dioxide [CO_2] emissions are causing the Earth to trap and retain too much heat. If that's true, they say, then we must immediately begin to curtail carbon emissions. Environmentalist "journalists" in the UK have gone so far as to begin calling for a war effort against industrial emissions of carbon dioxide. On December 4, [2007] in the British newspaper *The Guardian*, George Monbiot said, for instance: "We must confront a challenge that is as great and as pressing as the rise of the Axis powers. Had we thrown up our hands then, as many people are tempted to do today, you would be reading this paper in German." The new climate-change war effort, he continued, will require putting government in charge of the economy and drastically curtailing modern lifestyles. "The US economy," he said, "was spun round on a dime in 1942 as civilian manufacturing was switched to military production. The state took on greater powers than it had exercised before. Impossible policies suddenly became achievable."

Taking full control of the economy is exactly what the UN would like to do in order to curb carbon emissions. This, indeed, is an "impossible policy," but one made more likely if one buys into the idea that carbon emissions really are driving up global temperatures. The one problem in all of this, as *The Great Global Warming Swindle* shows, is that carbon emissions are very clearly not causing temperature increases.

Interviewing several scientific experts on the subject. Durkin's film points out that most of the warming of the last century occurred before 1940 and that the world cooled for decades following World War II. Professor Syun-lchi Akasofu, director of the International Arctic Research Center, is one expert Durkin interviewed on the subject. In the film, the scientist notes: "CO_2 began to increase exponentially in about 1940. But, the temperature actually began to decrease in 1940 and continued until about 1975." This is clear and unmistakable evidence, he notes, that CO_2 is not causing climate change. "When the CO_2 is increasing rapidly, but yet the temperature decreasing," he pointed out in the film, "then we can not say that CO_2 and the temperature go together."

Quite to the contrary, it seems that warming causes an increase in carbon dioxide; carbon dioxide does not cause an increase in warming. In fact, as the film notes, the ice-core record very clearly shows that CO_2 increases in the atmosphere follow centuries after temperature increases. In the film, paleoclimatologist Ian Clark of the University of Ottawa makes this point, looking at a graph of ice-core data. "We see temperature going up from early time to later time at a very key interval when we came out of a glaciation. We see the temperature going up and then we see the CO_2 coming up. CO_2 lags behind that increase—it's got an 800-year lag—so temperature is leading CO_2 by 800 years."

Climate Change Is Not the Greatest Threat to the World's Poor

Climate—or more accurately, weather—remains one of the greatest challenges facing the poor. Climate change adds nothing to that calculus, however. Climate and weather patterns have always changed, as they always will. Man has always best dealt with this through wealth creation and technological advance—a.k.a. adaptation—and most poorly through superstitious casting of blame, such as burning "witches." The wealthiest societies have always adapted best. One would prefer to face a similar storm in Florida than Bangladesh. Institutions, infrastructure and affordable energy are key to dealing with an ever-changing climate, not rationing energy.

Christopher Horner,
"Top 10 'Global Warming' Myths,"
Human Events, *February 20, 2007.*

It Could Be Warmer

In fact, as Clark and others point out in the film, it is not now as warm as it has been in the past. Within the last 1,000 years, in fact, there was a period known as the Medieval Warm Period when the climate was warmer than it is today. The film doesn't make the connection, but it is interesting to ponder the fact, nonetheless, that the height of the Medieval Warm Period was, give or take a few years, 800 years ago. Given the time lag between temperature increases and atmospheric CO_2 increases, we shouldn't be surprised to see increases in CO_2 today.

Naturally, this kind of analysis does not sit well with radical environmentalists, and *The Great Global Warming Swindle* has its share of critics. Alleging that Durkin was guilty of misrepresenting certain facts in the film, in April [2007], 37 scientists signed their names to an open letter to the filmmaker objecting "to plans ... to distribute DVD versions" of the film. Rather disingenuously, they claimed that they were not "seeking the censorship of differing viewpoints or the curtailment of free speech," though, in fact, that is exactly what they were seeking.

Durkin, for his part, has vigorously defended his work. In a response to critics published in the *London Telegraph*, he responded: "The remarkable thing is not that I was attacked. But that the attacks have been so feeble." Continuing, he noted: "Too many journalists and scientists have built their careers on the global-warming alarm. Certain newspapers have staked their reputation on it. The death of this theory will be painful and ugly. But it will die. Because it is wrong, wrong, wrong."

Finally, with the release of *The Great Global Warming Swindle* on DVD, American audiences get the chance to judge for themselves. It's a good bet that most will come away from the film convinced that Durkin is right about global warming.

> "Overpopulation by the human species, our continuing exponential birth rate and our lack of a biocentric worldview are having far-reaching and over-whelmingly destructive impacts."

Overpopulation Threatens the Environment

Gedden Cascadia

Human overpopulation is having a destructive impact on the environment, asserts environmental activist Gedden Cascadia in the following viewpoint. As the population grows, so does its need for resources, he maintains. Because the Earth has limited resources, when the human population exceeds the Earth's carrying capacity—the maximum number any vessel can carry—environmental degradation is inevitable, Cascadia argues. Those who care about the Earth and the creatures that inhabit it should not have children, he reasons.

As you read, consider the following questions:

1. How does Albert Barlett illustrate the effects of exponential growth?

Gedden Cascadia, "A Few Too Many," *Earth First! Journal*, May/June 2008, p. 22. Copyright © 2008 Daily Planet Publishing. Reproduced by permission.

2. In Cascadia's view, what was the only event that had a marked impact on human population growth?

3. What does the author report happened to the Anasazi civilization?

Snip. A simple action that any guy can have done. Snip. One moment in time that will solidify a person's resolve to help the planet. Vasectomy. The most liberating moment of a man's life is when the vas deferens tubes are severed and the planet is spared the burden of one more resource-draining, Earth-trampling shit machine.

Not to sound overly harsh, but let's face the facts: Overpopulation by the human species, our continuing exponential birth rate and our lack of a biocentric worldview are having far-reaching and overwhelmingly destructive impacts on many other animal and plant species. Every species on this planet has a finite amount of time to exist before the inevitable fate of extinction creeps up on it. The thing that differs in the current state of affairs is that this latest round of global extinctions is not being caused by outside forces (meteors) or gradual changes in the planet's climate (ice ages), but rather by a single species: humans. This species is fully aware of what it is doing and has the capacity to stop the destruction if only it wanted to.

Exponential Growth

As of 9 p.m. Pacific Standard Time, on March 31, 2008, the estimated world population is 6,658,448,807 and growing, according to the US Census Bureau. The human species is increasing in an exponential fashion. There is a story by Albert Bartlett that clearly illustrates the effect of exponential growth: "Imagine a hypothetical strain of bacteria in which each bacterium divides into two every 60 seconds (the doubling time is one minute). Assume that one bacterium is put in a bottle at 11 a.m. The bottle (its world) is full at noon." At 11:59, the bottle was only half full, and at 11:58, the bottle was 75 percent empty. If the bacterium was capable of realizing that it was running out of room, at what point do you think it would have made that discovery? At 11:59, when half of the world was empty? Possibly. At 11:58, when only one-quarter of the world was populated? Probably not. If the bacteria was able to escape its world and move into three new bottles, it would have bought itself only two more minutes before its world was once more packed full.

The human growth rate is 1.2 percent per year. This certainly doesn't seem like much of a number. It is significantly lower than the rate of the fictional bacteria. However, even at such a low rate, we are doubling the world's population in less than 50 years. This means that there are 84 million more people on this planet every year—230,000 more every day. This is not the number of births. This is the actual amount of increase—almost 10,000 more people every hour. There were 2,819 deaths reported as a result of the September 11, 2001 attacks on the World Trade Center in New York City. In fewer than 20 minutes, the world population had recovered. The tsunami that hit Asia in December 2004, killing 230,000 people, only impacted the world's population for a day before the numbers were once again the same. Such events are little more than speed bumps on our race to overpopulate. When looking at the graph of population growth, the only event that had a marked impact on human population was the Black Death, and even that shows up as a barely perceivable dimple.

The Human Footprint

As the population grows, not surprisingly, the amount of resources we must take from the Earth grows as well. Most arable land is now occupied. Humanity has to go farther and farther afield to find the resources it craves. It wasn't that long ago that the thought of drilling for oil in an arctic environment would have been dismissed as an absurdity. Yet here we

The Price for Each Human

Much of our environmental problem is due to overpopulation. There are simply too many people for the planet to sustain—at least the way we expect to be sustained. Each new person requires more food, water and oxygen. At the same time, each is producing more carbon dioxide, carbon monoxide and methane (the big culprits of global warming). For each additional human, planet Earth (and the rest of us) pays a price. The world knows where this is all headed. In fact, we even devote an *entire* day—Earth Day.

Oliver "Buzz" Thomas,
"Might Our Religion Be Killing Us?"
USA Today, *April 21, 2008.*

are, engaged in heated debate about the preservation of the Arctic National Wildlife Refuge. The ever-increasing need for natural resources to support an out-of-control population is driving the development of more extreme measures to secure those once out-of-reach fragments left over from the first wave of extractions.

How many people can the Earth support in a sustainable manner? No one knows. The estimates range from a few million to more than 40 billion people. One thing is certain: As we expand, we are actively destroying the Earth's biodiversity. This trend is not new. As the first people migrated across the landscape, they left a swath of extinctions behind them. As soon as humanity reached the North American continent some 10,000 years ago, we see in the fossil record evidence of the extinction of all megafauna on the continent. Is this nothing more than a coincidence? Not according to a growing number of anthropologists, who attribute the missing mammals to humans overhunting them. The entire history of humanity is one of environmental destruction and the eradication of other species. This was true when the entire world's population of hominids was only a few million. What else can we expect from a population of several billion?

The Environment's Carrying Capacity

If a population overshoots the carrying capacity of its environment, then the population will crash until it is realigned with the carrying capacity. However, if in the process of overshooting, environmental degradation takes place, the new carrying capacity will be greatly reduced, if not gone altogether. In isolated communities, overshoot can manifest itself on a local level. In his book *Collapse*, Jared Diamond gives extensive examples of societies that have suffered greatly and, in many cases, disappeared entirely because of their impacts on the surrounding environment. The Anasazi, of what is now considered the Southwest US, are one such example. Having wreaked havoc upon the land as they increased soil salinity with improper irrigation practices, they could no longer support a growing population, and their society subsequently disappeared because of it.

Humanity is now at the point where civilizations are no longer isolated. We are a global species with one global society and, more and more, one global culture. Our destruction is no longer limited to one region or one continent. Everything we do has global ramifications, the likes of which have never been seen before. There is a very real chance that we have already overshot the carrying capacity of the Earth. Only time will tell. There is little chance of us actually physically destroying the Earth, but we seem to be doing our best to destroy our ability (and the ability of countless other species) to live on it. The most important question may not be how we as a species can survive but rather if we as a species *should* survive.

A Destructive Choice

The most environmentally destructive act any one person can do is to have a child. However, the need for progeny is hardwired in most species on this planet, and it may seem unnatural to forsake this desire in the name of environmentalism. The answer is simple. The answer is as abundant as there are children needing homes, families and someone to love them. The point of this essay is not to be anti-family, anti-parent or anti-child. Adoption is the logical course of action for anyone who wants to be a parent but does not want to contribute to the destruction of the Earth. There is nothing so special about any individual's DNA that makes it more important than the thousands of lives every additional human will snuff out. When comparing the cost of adoption with the cost of breeding in the US, it can be much cheaper to adopt than give birth. There are many agencies that help with the financial aspect of adoption. People who are shallow enough to insist on a little white baby are going to pay more, but if your motivations are nobler than some perceived aesthetic of your new child, the cost drops dramatically.

The conclusion is simple. If an individual cares about the Earth or the animals—hell, even if that person cares about other people—they will not breed. Abstinence and same-sex partners are great, but the finality and commitment implied by a vasectomy or tubal ligation make a true hero.

> "Rules, laws, and customs that enhance
> markets and economic freedom will im-
> prove human welfare and environmen-
> tal quality making overpopulation a
> minor problem."

Overpopulation Does Not Threaten the Environment

Ross B. Emmett

*Overpopulation poses no threat to the environment because hu-
man ingenuity and free markets will restrain population growth,
claims Ross B. Emmett in the following viewpoint. Indeed, in the
early 1800s, political economist Robert Malthus believed that
marriage and economic freedom would lead people to have fewer
children, Emmett maintains. And, rather than develop policies
that run counter to human nature, Emmett argues, policies that
promote human invention and economic growth will prevent
overpopulation and threats to environmental quality. Emmett is
a political theory professor at Michigan State University.*

As you read, consider the following questions:

1. According to Emmett, why was Malthus no Scrooge?

Ross B. Emmett, "Malthus Reconsidered: Population, Natural Resources, and Markets,"
PERC Policy Series, December 2006. Reproduced by permission.

2. Who does the author claim are the two leading individuals in the modern population debate?

3. In the author's opinion, what is the difference between a "constrained" and an "unconstrained" vision of human nature?

Robert Malthus [political economist of the 18th and 19th centuries] is often reputed to be a Scrooge. Readers will recall that when the miserly merchant from "A Christmas Carol" was asked for a charitable donation for the poor, he replied: "If they [the poor] would rather die . . . they had better do it, and decrease the surplus population."

The Population Debate

"Surplus population:" That sums up the common perception of Malthus' population principle. The world has too many people and because food production cannot keep up with procreation, people will starve. The name Malthus is frequently invoked in modern environmental debates. Those who believe we are running out of resources and need to act swiftly to prevent an eventual population and environmental apocalypse are often called neo-Malthusians. They acknowledge Malthus as the first spokesman for concern about overpopulation.

Countering this view is a group I call neo-institutionalists. As exemplified by Julian Simon [a 20th-century professor of business], they believe that human ingenuity and the expansion of free markets have made the world a better place and reduced overpopulation to a minor problem, if it is a problem at all. They often criticize the neo-Malthusians with a reference to Malthus' Scrooge-like reputation.

However, Malthus was no Scrooge. His concern for the poor and support for policies benefiting all members of society are amply reflected in his work. The reputation he carries today is a distortion of his population theory, a slant created by his nineteenth-century opponents. . . . His population principle was the starting point for a policy that promoted economic freedom. His outlook toward human progress was one of cautious optimism, rather than the cynicism we associate with Scrooge. Taken together, his ideas are closer to the neo-institutionalist position in the current debate than they are to the neo-Malthusian view.

Since the publication of [Paul Ehrlich's] *The Population Bomb* [in 1968], the debate over human population and the environment has been cast as a battle between pessimists, the neo-Malthusians, and optimists, the neo-institutionalists. Neo-Malthusians fear the "trap" of what they call overpopulation. They believe humanity will fall into it unless we undergo a change in values that will lead us to have fewer children and consume less. In contrast, neo-institutionalists believe that the rules, laws, and customs that enhance markets and economic freedom will improve human welfare and environmental quality making overpopulation a minor problem—if a problem at all. Two leading individuals in this debate are Paul Ehrlich, for the neo-Malthusians, and the late Julian Simon, for the neo-institutionalists.

The Neo-Malthusians

Neo-Malthusians do not normally label themselves as such (the label is given by others), but they see themselves as Malthus' intellectual descendants. In their book *Betrayal of Science and Reason*, Paul and Anne Ehrlich state: "Ever since Reverend Thomas Malthus at the end of the eighteenth century warned about the dangers of overpopulation, analysts have been concerned about maintaining a balance between human numbers and the human food supply. That concern remains valid today."

Humanity must recognize that "exponential growth never can go on very long in a finite space with finite resources" and therefore that growth must be curbed. On that basis, neo-Malthusians advocate short- and long-term policies.

In the short term, they propose government controls to restrain population and consumption. In [their 2004 book] *One with Nineveh*, Paul and Anne Ehrlich favor policies that promote birth control, remove explicit and implicit government incentives to have or maintain larger families, expand access to abortion services, and impose penalties on parents who exceed a mandated family size. They also want governments to bring market prices in line with the cost that, in their view, human consumption imposes on the environment.

These policies are designed to intervene directly in markets and private lives to bring incentives in line with sustainable values. Direct intervention is required, neo-Malthusians argue, because fundamental change in priorities takes a long time.

The long-term neo-Malthusian policy goal is a change of heart. Human nature must be reformed by changing people's values. "We are asking for ... a cultural change," Ehrlich said in an article co-authored with the editor of *Science*.

In his book *Human Natures*, Ehrlich amplified his view of cultural change. The underlying genetic makeup provides the palette upon which human nature is formed, but it is given shape and form by culture—different sets of cultural values represent alternative paths of human evolution. Because humans can consciously choose to alter their values, people can change the direction of human evolution. "Conscious cultural evolution," the Ehrlichs call it. If humans are to escape the population trap permanently, neo-Malthusians argue, they need to reform human nature by a process of cultural change that will lead us to adopt "sustainable" values.

The Neo-Institutionalists

Refusing to accept the pessimism of the neo-Malthusians, neo-institutionalists argue that a market-based free society can balance the growth of population and the economy and continue to improve environmental quality. They are called neo-

Preventing Famine and Environmental Degredation

If the right social institutions are lacking—democratic governance, secure private property, free markets—it is possible for a nation to fall into the ... trap of rising poverty and increasing environmental degradation. The economies of many countries in Africa are declining, not because of high population growth rates or lack of resources, but because they have failed to implement the basic policies for encouraging economic growth: namely, widespread education, secure property rights and democratic governance.

Democratic governance and open markets have in fact proved indispensable for the prevention of famine in modern times. Nobel Prize-winning economist Amartya Sen notes that "in the terrible history of famines in the world, there is hardly any case in which a famine has occurred in a country that is independent and democratic, with an uncensored press."

Ronald A. Bailey, *"The Law of Increasing Returns,"*
National Interest, *Spring 2000.*

institutionalists because they focus on the laws, rules, and cus-toms—the institutions—that guide human behavior. Neo-institutionalists believe that we should take humans as we find them and it is preferable to allow people to be free in an insti-tutional framework that encourages market activity. They do not believe that basic human nature changes.

Neo-institutionalists make two arguments that link popu-lation growth, economic growth, and environmental quality through institutions. The first is that economic growth, which depends on market institutions, can lower fertility rates and, hence, restrain population growth. Early in the current debate, Julian Simon showed that increases in per capita income, which are a result of economic growth, lead to decreased births per married woman. Thus, he argued, direct control of population, which is an intrusion on free choice, is unnecessary.

The second neo-institutionalist argument is that human ingenuity will offset the few adverse effects of population growth. Simon argued that people are the "ultimate resource" because of their ingenuity. The neo-Malthusians underestimate the creative power of humans; technological change will ensure that production keeps pace with population. The population trap is no trap at all because humans creatively respond to market incentives, expanding the resource base available for productive uses. While population growth means more people to feed, it also means that we have more people to devote their creativity and imagination to solving the problems of transforming resources into useful goods and services. "It is your mind that matters economically, as much as or more than your mouth or hands [according to Simon]." Echoing Simon, neo-institutionalists point out that the institutions that encourage the use of our ingenuity—free markets and property rights—are the same ones that promote economic growth.

Thus, neo-institutionalist policies focus on institutions and the consequences of reform, rather than on the reform of human nature. When societies create institutions that allow people to pursue their values freely in markets under a rule of law, decisions about fertility, innovation, and resource use will be balanced in ways that enhance economic growth, moderate population growth, and improve environmental quality. Simon put the consequences succinctly: "The standard of living has risen along with the size of the world's population since the beginning of recorded time. There is no convincing economic reason why these trends toward a better life should not continue indefinitely."

Malthus and the Population Principle

In his own day, Malthus kicked off an emotional dispute about human nature and the improvement of society that lasted through the nineteenth century. He was on the opposite side of this debate than we might expect if we focused only on his famous population principle or the Malthusian label. Historian Arnold Toynbee once called this nineteenth-century debate the "bitter dispute between economists and human beings." Malthus was in the company of the economists, not the "human beings."

At the center of the dispute was the claim made by Adam Smith, Malthus, and other economists such as John Stuart Mill that any real prospects for social improvement depended upon policies that accepted human beings as they are, with all their differences and imperfections, not as idealists hoped they might be. This approach has been called a "constrained vision" by Thomas Sowell [in his 2002 book, *A Conflict of Visions: Ideological Origins of Political Struggles*].

The economists' opponents, operating under what Sowell calls an "unconstrained vision," and acting as self-declared spokespersons for "human beings," argued that society could only be improved if human nature changed. They assumed that markets could not contribute to a good social order because market interactions allowed selfish interests to control society. These opponents, such as Robert Owen, John Bray, Thomas Carlyle, John Ruskin, and Charles Kingsley, did not favor economic freedom. Instead, they sought to introduce socialist utopias or to hold onto one form or another of feudalism (including, for the likes of Carlyle and Ruskin, the race-based feudalism of the American South), or to school people in what it meant to be "truly" human. Eventually, as the theory of evolution began to be recognized, some of the nineteenth-century spokespersons for "humanity" even turned to selective breeding and other eugenic practices to improve human nature.

Smith, Malthus, and the other economists believed that the potential for changing human nature was small. But they also thought that more freedom was possible by working within the constraints of human nature than could be accomplished by attempting to overcome the constraints. They wanted to change the incentives people faced, not people's inherent nature. The economists of Malthus' era, therefore, promoted the expansion of property rights, free markets, and customs that enabled free choices.

Malthus' population theory was an important part of the economists' argument. In their view, human societies will overrun their natural resources if they do not have the right kind of institutions. But that will not happen in societies that have property rights, markets, and some means (for example, marriage) of ensuring that fathers are responsible for the costs of rearing their own children. In such societies, economic growth and moderate population growth can be sustained indefinitely, bringing steadily rising real incomes to everyone....

The Institutions That Promote Restraint

Malthus' opposition to the reform proposals of his day (and ours) led his opponents to say that he "condemned the worker to death from starvation, and to celibacy" [as quoted in Karl Marx's *Theories of Surplus Value*]. Those with unconstrained visions of human nature have been unable to see how his ideas could translate into anything more than "gloomy presentiments" [as quoted in Robert Heilbroner's *The Worldly Philosophers*]. The fact that Malthus emphasized the constraints of human nature and the "black train of distresses" avoided by the exercise of restraint have distracted attention away from his interest in institutional reform.

Yet he was right about many things, even though he is not appreciated for them today. He recognized that institutions such as marriage, property rights, and markets lead people to practice prudential restraint, lowering fertility rates and yielding the prospect of steadily rising real incomes. These institutions—property rights, free markets, and marriage—ensure that individuals make wise decisions regarding their resources. Production will be sufficient to meet the effective demands of the population.

Malthus opposed interventionist policies that restricted freedom. Improving society was tricky business. For the most part, he trusted institutions that people voluntarily created to encourage their exercise of prudential restraint. He saw reform of government policies as possible, especially through the elimination of rules and laws that restricted market activity, mobility, and access.

The Positive Effects of Free Choice

Assuming that the institutions of property rights and marriage were in place, market-enhancing reforms would create an institutional framework in which people's free choices could be trusted to have positive social consequences. "If . . . we come to the conclusion, not to interfere in any respect, but to leave every man to his own free choice, and responsible only to God for the evil he does . . . this is all I contend for" he wrote. [Malthus continued,] "I would on no account do more; but I contend, that at present we are very far from doing this."

In the nineteenth-century debate between economists and the spokespersons for removing the chains that constrained human nature, Malthus' name was invoked in the same breath as those of Adam Smith, John Stuart Mill, and the other great economists. In the modern debate, Malthus' namesakes are, ironically, the ones urging us to reject the neo-institutionalist view that institutions underlie the economic freedom that has brought prosperity and better environmental quality. It is time to put Malthus back in his rightful place in the modern debate.

Periodical Bibliography

The following articles have been selected to supplement the diverse views presented in this chapter.

Tom Arrandale	"Disappearing Species," *CQ Researcher*, November 30, 2007.
Michael Barone	"A Step Back from Enviro Lunacy," *American Enterprise*, July 28, 2008.
Jerry A. Coyne and Hopi E. Hoekstra	"The Greatest Dying, a Fate Worse Than Global Warming," *New Republic*, September 24, 2007.
David A. Fahrenthold	"Climate Change Brings More Risk of Extinctions," *Washington Post*, September 17, 2007.
John Feeney	"Return of the Population Timebomb," *Guardian [United Kingdom]*, May 5, 2008.
James Kanter	"UN Issues 'Final Wake-Up Call' on Population and Environment," *International Herald Tribune*, October 25, 2007.
Patrick J. Michaels	"The Grand Exaggerator," *National Review [Online]*, July 24, 2008.
Stephen Moore	"Clear-Eyed Optimists: The World Is Getting Better, Though No One Likes to Hear It," *Wall Street Journal*, October 5, 2007.
Samuel Thernstrom	"Gore's Climate Claptrap," *Real Clear Politics*, July 25, 2008.
Rick Weiss	"Report Urges Huge Changes to Factory-Farming Practices," *Seattle Times*, April 30, 2008.
Elizabeth Williamson	"Farms May Be Exempted from Emission Rules," *Washington Post*, February 26, 2008.

OPPOSING
VIEWPOINTS®
SERIES

CHAPTER 2

How Should Global Warming Be Addressed?

Chapter Preface

Few experts today dispute that global warming is a real threat. Global temperatures today are more than 1 degree Fahrenheit warmer than they were at the beginning of the twentieth century, and the increase has been greatest in recent years. Montana's Glacier National Park boasted 150 glaciers when the park was created in 1920. That number has fallen to fewer than 30. The snows of Mount Kilimanjaro in Tanzania have melted 80 percent since 1912, and many claim that these symbolic snows could disappear by 2020. "The climate is changing, and the rate of change as projected exceeds anything seen in nature in the past 10,000 years," claims James Hurrell, director of the Climate and Global Dynamics Division at the National Center for Atmospheric Research. "Greenhouse gas concentrations in the atmosphere are now higher than at any time in the last 750,000 years," Hurrell maintains. While few analysts debate the reality of global climate change, some do dispute whether the impact will be severe enough to justify the enormous costs of efforts to reduce it. Indeed, whether the United States should ratify the Kyoto Protocol, an international treaty that mandates limits on carbon emissions to reduce greenhouse gases by 5 percent by 2012, is the subject of rigorous debate.

Supporters of the Kyoto Protocol argue that the impact of global warming will be considerable, therefore justifying significant measures to reduce greenhouse gas emissions. "[G]lobal warming will be disruptive in many, many ways," Hurrell maintains, with the potential to cause "drought, heat waves, wildland fires and flooding." Europe, which in 2003 experienced a heat wave that killed more than 25,000 people, has embraced the Kyoto Protocol. According to George Marshall, British environmentalist and member of the activist organization Rising Tide, "We have no right . . . to argue to future generations ... that we were waiting to achieve a full scientific understanding" before acting. Vermont Senator James Jeffords believes strongly that the United States also should join the treaty, arguing, "The U.S. has been and remains the largest emitter of greenhouse gases. It has a responsibility to its own people and to the people of the world to be a leader on this issue."

Kyoto Protocol opponents claim that there is no real evidence that the impact of global warming will be as severe as supporters suggest. Stephen Milloy, a scholar at the libertarian Cato Institute, warns that implementing the rigorous precautionary policies of the Kyoto Protocol before clear evidence of a threat could result in "regulation based on irrational fears." Some opponents add that the costs of trying to achieve the Protocol's carbon emission limits will outweigh any benefits. Regulation, these analysts assert, could seriously damage the U.S. economy. "Mandatory reduction of carbon dioxide ... could effectively throw our nation into an economic depression," maintains Oklahoma Senator James Inhofe. Still others are concerned that the Protocol standards are too optimistic. Even if all participating nations were to meet their initial Protocol targets, they claim, global emissions would not drop enough to affect climate change. The first round of cuts "doesn't even begin to address the problem," says University of California, Berkeley, physics professor Richard A. Miller.

Whether the Kyoto Protocol is an effective strategy to reduce global warming remains to be seen. The authors in the following chapter debate the effectiveness of other global warming reduction strategies.

"We need to make the transition to renewable energy—away from fossil fuels—quickly in order to enable clean
and sustainable growth."

Renewable Energy Can Reduce the Impact of Global Warming

Sven Teske, Arthouros Zervos, and Oliver Schäfer

Renewable energy sources are necessary to address the threat posed by global warming, argue Sven Teske, Arthouros Zervos, and Oliver Schäfer in the following viewpoint. In fact, the authors claim, many nations currently use renewable sources with great success. Renewables are not only cheaper, but they also produce fewer carbon emissions and reduce dependence on fossil fuels, the authors maintain. Because coal plants are aging and the demand for energy is growing, the time to employ renewable energy is now, the authors reason. Teske represents Greenpeace International; Zervos and Schäfer represent the European Renewable Energy Council.

As you read, consider the following questions:

1. According to Teske, Zervos and Schäfer, what are the problems with current electricity generation?

Sven Teske, Arthouros Zervos, and Oliver Schäfer, "The Energy [r]evolution," In *Energy [r]evolution: A Blueprint for Solving Global Warming*, Greenpeace International and European Renewable Energy Council (EREC), January 2007. Copyright © 2007 Greenpeace. Reproduced by permission.

2. In the authors' view, how should practices address the impact of climate change on the poorest communities?

3. What figures do the authors cite to illustrate the current contribution of renewable energy sources?

The climate change imperative demands nothing short of an energy [r]evolution. The expert consensus is that this fundamental change must begin very soon and well underway within the next ten years in order to avert the worst impacts. We do not need nuclear power. What we do need is a complete transformation in the way we produce, consume and distribute energy. Nothing short of such a revolution will enable us to limit global warming to less than 2° Celsius, above which the impacts become devastating.

Current electricity generation relies mainly on burning fossil fuels, with their associated CO_2 [carbon dioxide] emissions, in very large power stations which waste much of their primary input energy. More energy is lost as the power is moved around the electricity grid network and converted from high transmission voltage down to a supply suitable for domestic or commercial consumers. The system is innately vulnerable to disruption: localised technical, weather-related or even deliberately caused faults can quickly cascade, resulting in widespread blackouts. Whichever technology is used to generate electricity within this old fashioned configuration, it will inevitably be subject to some, or all, of these problems. At the core of the energy [r]evolution therefore, there needs to be a change in the way that energy is both produced and distributed.

The Mechanisms of Energy Sustainability

The energy [r]evolution can be achieved by adhering to five key principles:

1. *Implement clean, renewable solutions and decentralise energy systems.* There is no energy shortage. All we need to

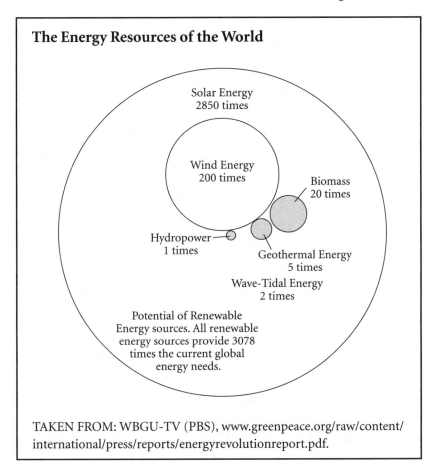

The Energy Resources of the World

Solar Energy
2850 times

Wind Energy
200 times

Biomass
20 times

Hydropower
1 times

Geothermal Energy
5 times

Wave-Tidal Energy
2 times

Potential of Renewable
Energy sources. All renewable
energy sources provide 3078
times the current global
energy needs.

TAKEN FROM: WBGU-TV (PBS), www.greenpeace.org/raw/content/
international/press/reports/energyrevolutionreport.pdf.

do is use existing technologies to harness energy effectively and efficiently. Renewable energy and energy efficiency measures are ready, viable and increasingly competitive. Wind, solar and other renewable energy technologies have experienced double digit market growth for the past decade.

Just as climate change is real, so is the renewable energy sector. Sustainable decentralised energy systems produce less carbon emissions, are cheaper and involve less dependence on imported fuel. They create more jobs and empower local communities. Decentralised systems are more secure and more efficient. This is what the energy [r]evolution must aim to create.

2. *Respect natural limits.* We must learn to respect natural limits. There is only so much carbon that the atmosphere can absorb. Each year we emit about 23 billion tonnes of CO_2; we are literally filling up the sky. Geological resources of coal could provide several 100 years of fuel, but we cannot burn them and keep within safe limits. Oil and coal development must be ended.

To stop the earth's climate spinning out of control, most of the world's fossil fuel reserves—coal, oil and gas—must remain in the ground. Our goal is for humans to live within the natural limits of our small planet.

3. *Phase out dirty, unsustainable energy.* We need to phase out coal and nuclear power. We cannot continue to build coal plants at a time when emissions pose a real and present danger to both ecosystems and people. And we cannot continue to fuel the myriad nuclear threats by pretending nuclear power can in any way help to combat climate change. There is no role for nuclear power in the energy [r]evolution.

4. *Equity and fairness.* As long as there are natural limits, there needs to be a fair distribution of benefits and costs within societies, between nations and between present and future generations. At one extreme, a third of the world's population has no access to electricity, whilst the most industrialised countries consume much more than their fair share.

The effects of climate change on the poorest communities are exacerbated by massive global energy inequality. If we are to address climate change, one of the principles must be equity and fairness, so that the benefits of energy services—such as light, heat, power and transport—are available for all: north and south, rich and poor. Only in this way can we create true energy security, as well as the conditions for genuine human security.

5. *Decouple growth from fossil fuel use.* Starting in the developed countries, economic growth must fully decouple from fossil fuels. It is a fallacy to suggest that economic growth must be predicated on their increased combustion.

- We need to use the energy we produce much more efficiently.

- We need to make the transition to renewable energy—away from fossil fuels—quickly in order to enable clean and sustainable growth.

From Principles to Practice

Today, renewable energy sources account for 13% of the world's primary energy demand. Biomass, which is mainly used for heating, is the main renewable energy source. The share of renewable energy in electricity generation is 18%. The contribution of renewables to primary energy demand for heat supply is around 26%. About 80% of primary energy supply today still comes from fossil fuels, and the remaining 7% from nuclear power.

The time is right to make substantial structural changes in the energy and power sector within the next decade. Many power plants in industrialised countries, such as the USA, Japan and the European Union, are nearing retirement; more than half of all operating power plants are over 20 years old. At the same time developing countries, such as China, India and Brazil, are looking to satisfy the growing energy demand created by expanding economies.

Within the next ten years, the power sector will decide how this new demand will be met, either by fossil and nuclear fuels or by the efficient use of renewable energy. The energy [r]evolution scenario is based on a new political framework in favour of renewable energy and cogeneration combined with energy efficiency.

To make this happen both renewable energy and co-generation—on a large scale and through decentralised, smaller units—have to grow faster than overall global energy demand. Both approaches must replace old generation and deliver the additional energy required in the developing world.

> *"While renewable energy is relatively environmentally friendly, it does leave a footprint. Its appetite for land is striking."*

Renewable Energy's Usefulness in Reducing Global Warming Is Limited

Lyndon Thompson and Rory J. Clarke

Renewable energy sources are not yet adequate to meet the rising demand for energy, assert Lyndon Thompson and Rory J. Clarke in the following viewpoint. Because research and development is costly, renewables would not be as useful in developing countries as would cheap, conventional sources, they argue. Moreover, the authors claim, renewables also have an impact on the environment—ethanol reduces soil quality and hydroelectric power emits carbon dioxide (CO_2). Thompson is a professor at the University of the West of England in Bristol; Clarke is editor of OECD Observer, *a publication of the Organisation for Economic Cooperation and Development.*

Lyndon Thompson and Rory J. Clarke, "Renewable Promise," *OECD Observer*, December 2006, pp. 20–21. Copyright © 2006 OECD Publications and Information Centre. Reproduced by permission.

As you read, consider the following questions:

1. What do Thompson and Clarke claim are the main renewable energy sources?
2. How is methane generated and what is its impact on global warming, in the authors' opinion?
3. According to the authors, who benefits from the fact that renewable energy is in vogue?

Global electricity demand is growing rapidly. Demand for transport energy is also rising. Renewable energy is as yet not capable of matching the energy-density of fossil fuels, and it absorbs a lot of land, whether for cultivating biofuels or laying out solar panels. From solar to hydro, renewable sources are also unevenly distributed and supply can be irregular.

The Contribution of Renewable Energy

Nevertheless, technology and know-how are improving and renewable energy sources have already started to contribute more to the overall energy mix. Together with policies and other developments on the demand side, in business and households, these could make for a healthier outlook for 2030.

The main renewable energy sources are hydropower, biomass and waste, wind, geothermal, solar, and tide and wave-generated energy. Hydropower and biomass are the most exploited sources today and the use of wind power is growing fast. In 2004, these renewables, including biofuels for transport, accounted for around 13% of total world primary energy demand.

The impact on electricity generation is noteworthy: renewables in 2004 accounted for some 18% of total terawatt hours generated and, according to the IEA's [International Energy Agency] *World Energy Outlook [WEO] 2006*, will account for 21% in 2030 on current policies. With extra investment and stronger policies and measures, that share rises to 26% in the report's alternative policy scenario, and could climb even higher.

Hydropower accounts for most renewable electricity generation, with a 16% share of total power generated in 2030, compared with less than 10% for all other renewable sources. Some hydropower is under-exploited, with only a third of potential now tapped globally. Extra expansion could take place in the developing world. But capacity constraints mean hydro's share in total electricity supply in the IEA's alternative scenario for 2030 would not increase much, even if new policies are adopted. The contribution from other renewables would be nearly eight times higher than now, thanks in large part to an expansion in wind power and biomass. Wind's contribution in the alternative policy scenario rises by over a fifth compared with the IEA's business-as-usual reference scenario.

In fact, such is the room for efficiency improvements in energy use that we could achieve far more from less. Overall electricity generation would be 12% lower in the alternative, yet quite-feasible scenario for 2030 than under a business-as-usual outlook if measures were adopted on the demand side, from fitting better light bulbs to improving house and office building construction. The share of oil, for instance, slides from 7% of electricity generation in 2004 to 2.9% in 2030.

These projections are realistic. The costs of research and development into improving technologies are high, but will fall as technology improves. This is already happening in the solar and wind markets, and in its alternative policy scenario, the 2006 *WEO* puts the investment cost of solar photovoltaic energy in 2030 at less than half the current figure. As over a quarter of new power-generating capacity will come from renewables, the cost of development is expected to reach $2,300 billion (in year 2005 dollars), or nearly half of power generation investment in the next 25 years.

The Limits of Renewables

There are limits to the promise of renewables, though. For one thing, developing countries will most likely be unable to

The Limits to Renewable Energy

There is much talk recently about the extent to which we can replace our dependence on fossil fuels with energy derived from renewable resources. While renewable energy holds great promise, there are some limitations to renewable forms of energy (as there are with anything) which are very widely proclaimed and generally used as "proof" that they can never solve all our problems. Obviously, we do not expect, nor desire, any single source of energy to be our sole and complete source; that would be foolish and dangerous. The more interesting question is how much of our demand the various forms can supply, and at what point in time will we reach the limit for each form.

Don Kopeckey, "The Limits to Renewable Energy,"
Energy Pulse, *May 2, 2008.*

use renewable alternatives on a large scale to leap-frog conventional energy sources such as coal to supply their future needs, unlike what some countries have been able to do in telecommunications with mobile phones, for instance. But renewables will still permit a better energy mix and could reduce usage of some of the less healthy forms of biomass, such as wood and charcoal burned in inefficient stoves, which the IEA points out kills nearly 2 million people every year. In any case, rapid economic growth in countries like India and China requires energy densities beyond the present scope of renewables. Both are starting to develop policies on renewable energy, in part to help curtail pollution.

While renewable energy is relatively environmentally friendly, it does leave a footprint. Its appetite for land is striking, even if conventional energy installations, like pipelines and oil refineries, also take up space. Biofuel production may mean fewer food crops, which in an age of rising populations could pose problems. Also, corn-based ethanol is particularly draining on soil quality and water resources. But while biofuels can achieve cleaner air by cutting emissions, as in Brazil, hybrid mixes are also to be found in "gas guzzlers" whose CO_2 emissions remain high compared with other vehicles.

As for hydroelectric power, even this emits large quantities of CO_2 and methane after a reservoir is initially flooded and submerged vegetation decays with changing water levels. Over time, new vegetation is engulfed and decomposes without oxygen, generating methane which the dam's turbines churn up into the atmosphere. The effect of methane on global warming is 21 times stronger than that of carbon dioxide. Also, though we know the environmental costs of burning fossil fuels, the side-effects of new energies are not fully understood. The impacts on local habitats or vegetation, or even climate patterns, of solar or wind power installations are still being documented. As tantalising and clean as it may be, renewable energy will probably not deliver a perfect world.

Still, renewable energy is in vogue, stimulating exciting expectations and business opportunities, not to mention high stock values. As ever, the countries with the right business frameworks seem to be benefiting first. In the UK [United Kingdom] where renewable energy has received early political support, the London Alternative Investment Market (AIM) already lists 20 companies with a combined market value of nearly £1.5bn ($2.9 bn). Wind and solar are attracting large corporations, too, including automotive and energy companies. British Petroleum (BP) says it intends to invest $1.8 billion in solar photovoltaic cells over the next three years. This is good news for the energy industry and small innovative firms, as well as for spin-offs in engineering, construction and conventional technology. Expect new companies to emerge and challenge incumbents, particularly large and unwieldy network providers, as lighter technologies bring energy supply to more local, flexible levels. Enabling regulation will be important.

Renewable energy is a promising technology, but as we warned in 2001 when dot-coms were expanding, hype should be resisted. The last e-bubble ended in tears. Global warming means it is in everyone's interest for a new e-economy based on renewable energy to take hold and stay a steady course.

| *"The risks of splitting atoms pale beside the dreadful toll exacted by fossil fuels."*

Nuclear Power Is the Best Way to Address Global Warming

Peter Schwartz and Spencer Reise

In the following viewpoint, Peter Schwartz and Spencer Reise contend that nuclear power is the best way to reduce dependence on fossil fuels and address global warming. Alternative energy sources such as water, wind, solar, and biomass are untested, they assert. Nuclear power, however, is proven technology that is being used worldwide, the authors maintain. Moreover, they claim that the disposal of nuclear waste and weapons proliferation are problems that are much easier to manage than global warming. Schwartz is chair of Global Business Network, a strategic-planning firm, and Reise writes about energy and technology issues for Wired.

As you read, consider the following questions:

1. What did a Harvard School of Public Health Study reveal about coal-burning electric power plants?

Peter Schwartz and Spencer Reise, "Nuclear Now!: How Clean, Green Atomic Energy Can Stop Global Warming," *WIRED*, vol. 13, February 2005. Copyright © 2005 Conde Nast Publications, Inc. All rights reserved. Reproduced by permission.

2. According to Schwartz and Reise, what have some of the world's most thoughtful green advocates discovered?

3. Which nations' activities do the authors cite as evidence that nuclear power is a thriving energy source?

On a cool spring morning a quarter century ago, a place in Pennsylvania called Three Mile Island exploded into the headlines and stopped the US nuclear power industry in its tracks. What had been billed as the clean, cheap, limitless energy source for a shining future was suddenly too hot to handle.

In the years since, we've searched for alternatives, pouring billions of dollars into windmills, solar panels, and biofuels. We've designed fantastically efficient lightbulbs, air conditioners, and refrigerators. We've built enough gas-fired generators to bankrupt California. But mainly, each year we hack 400 million more tons of coal out of Earth's crust than we did a quarter century before, light it on fire, and shoot the proceeds into the atmosphere.

The Consequences of Coal

The consequences aren't pretty. Burning coal and other fossil fuels is driving climate change, which is blamed for everything from western forest fires and Florida hurricanes to melting polar ice sheets and flooded Himalayan hamlets. On top of that, coal-burning electric power plants have fouled the air with enough heavy metals and other noxious pollutants to cause 15,000 premature deaths annually in the US alone, according to a Harvard School of Public Health study. Believe it or not, a coal-fired plant releases 100 times more radioactive material than an equivalent nuclear reactor—right into the air, too, not into some carefully guarded storage site. (And, by the way, more than 5,200 Chinese coal miners perished in accidents [in 2004]).

Burning hydrocarbons is a luxury that a planet with 6 billion energy-hungry souls can't afford. There's only one sane, practical alternative: nuclear power.

We now know that the risks of splitting atoms pale beside the dreadful toll exacted by fossil fuels. Radiation containment, waste disposal, and nuclear weapons proliferation are manageable problems in a way that global warming is not. Unlike the usual green alternatives—water, wind, solar, and biomass—nuclear energy is here, now, in industrial quantities. Sure, nuke plants are expensive to build—upward of $2 billion apiece—but they start to look cheap when you factor in the true cost to people and the planet of burning fossil fuels. And nuclear is our best hope for cleanly and efficiently generating hydrogen, which would end our other ugly hydrocarbon addiction—dependence on gasoline and diesel for transport.

Some of the world's most thoughtful greens have discovered the logic of nuclear power, including Gaia theorist James Lovelock, Greenpeace cofounder Patrick Moore, and Britain's Bishop Hugh Montefiore, a longtime board member of Friends of the Earth. Western Europe is quietly backing away from planned nuclear phaseouts. Finland has ordered a big reactor specifically to meet the terms of the Kyoto Protocol on climate change. China's new nuke plants—26 by 2025—are part of a desperate effort at smog control.

Even the shell-shocked US nuclear industry is coming out of its stupor. The 2001 report of Vice President Cheney's energy task force was only the most high profile in a series of pro-nuke developments. Nuke boosters are especially buoyed by more efficient plant designs, streamlined licensing procedures, and the prospect of federal subsidies.

In fact, new plants are on the way, however tentatively. Three groups of generating companies have entered a bureaucratic maze expected to lead to formal applications for plants by 2008. If everything breaks right, the first new reactors in decades will be online by 2014. If this seems ambitious, it's not; the industry hopes merely to hold on to nuclear's current 20 percent of the rapidly growing US electric power market.

That's not nearly enough. We should be shooting to match France, which gets 77 percent of its electricity from nukes. It's past time for a decisive leap out of the hydrocarbon era, time to send King Coal and, soon after, Big Oil shambling off to their well-deserved final resting places—maybe on a nostalgic old steam locomotive.

Besides, wouldn't it be a blast to barrel down the freeway in a hydrogen Hummer with a clean conscience as your copilot? Or not to feel like a planet killer every time you flick on the A/C [air conditioning]? That's how the future could be, if only we would get over our fear of the nuclear bogeyman and forge ahead—for real this time—into the atomic age.

The Demand for Energy

The granola crowd likes to talk about conservation and efficiency, and surely substantial gains can be made in those areas. But energy is not a luxury people can do without, like a gym membership or hair gel. The developed world built its wealth on cheap power—burning firewood, coal, petroleum, and natural gas, with carbon emissions the inevitable by product.

Indeed, material progress can be tracked in what gets pumped out of smokestacks. An hour of coal-generated 100-watt electric light creates 0.05 pounds of atmospheric carbon, a bucket of ice makes 0.3 pounds, an hour's car ride 5. The average American sends nearly half a ton of carbon spewing into the atmosphere every month. Europe and Japan are a little more economical, but even the most remote forest-burning peasants happily do their part.

And the worst—by far—is yet to come. An MIT [Massachusetts Institute of Technology] study forecasts that worldwide energy demand could triple by 2050. China could build a Three Gorges Dam every year forever and still not meet its

growing demand for electricity. Even the carbon reductions required by the Kyoto Protocol—which pointedly exempts developing countries like China—will be a drop in the atmospheric sewer.

The False Promise of Renewables

What is a rapidly carbonizing world to do? The high-minded answer, of course, is renewables. But the notion that wind, water, solar, or biomass will save the day is at least as fanciful as the once-popular idea that nuclear energy would be too cheap to meter. Jesse Ausubel, director of the human environment program at New York's Rockefeller University, calls renewable energy sources "false gods"—attractive but powerless. They're capital- and land-intensive, and solar is not yet remotely cost-competitive. Despite all the hype, tax breaks, and incentives, the proportion of US electricity production from renewables has actually fallen in the past 15 years, from 11.0 percent to 9.1 percent.

The decline would be even worse without hydropower, which accounts for 92 percent of the world's renewable electricity. While dams in the US are under attack from environmentalists trying to protect wild fish populations, the Chinese are building them on an ever grander scale. But even China's autocrats can't get past Nimby ["not in my backyard" opposition to the dams]. Stung by criticism of the monumental Three Gorges project—which required the forcible relocation of 1 million people—officials have suspended an even bigger project on the Nu Jiang River in the country's remote southwest. Or maybe someone in Beijing questioned the wisdom of reacting to climate change with a multibillion-dollar bet on rainfall.

Solar power doesn't look much better. Its number-one problem is cost: While the price of photovoltaic cells has been slowly dropping, solar-generated electricity is still four times more expensive than nuclear (and more than five times the cost of coal). Maybe someday we'll all live in houses with photovoltaic roof tiles, but in the real world, a run-of-the-mill 1,000-megawatt photovoltaic plant will require about 60 square miles of panes alone. In other words, the largest industrial structure ever built.

Wind is more promising, which is one reason it's the lone renewable attracting serious interest from big-time equipment manufacturers like General Electric. But even though price and performance are expected to improve, wind, like solar, is inherently fickle, hard to capture, and widely dispersed. And wind turbines take up a lot of space; Ausubel points out that the wind equivalent of a typical utility plant would require 300 square miles of turbines plus costly transmission lines from the wind-scoured fields of, say, North Dakota. Alternatively, there's California's Altamont Pass, where 5,400 windmills slice and dice some 1,300 birds of prey annually.

What about biomass? Ethanol is clean, but growing the amount of cellulose required to shift US electricity production to biomass would require farming—no wilting organics, please—an area the size of 10 Iowas.

Among fossil fuels, natural gas holds some allure; it emits a third as much carbon as coal. That's an improvement but not enough if you're serious about rolling back carbon levels. Washington's favorite solution is so-called clean coal, ballyhooed in stump speeches by both President [George W.] Bush (who offered a $2 billion research program) and [his 2004 presidential election campaign] challenger John Kerry (who upped the ante to $10 billion). But most of the work so far has been aimed at reducing acid rain by cutting sulphur dioxide and nitrogen oxide emissions, and more recently gasifying coal to make it burn cleaner. Actual zero-emissions coal is still a lab experiment that even fans say could double or triple generating costs. It would also leave the question of what to do with 1 million tons of extracted carbon each year.

The Growth of Nuclear Power

By contrast, nuclear power is thriving around the world despite decades of obituaries. Belgium derives 58 percent of its electricity from nukes, Sweden 45 percent, South Korea 40, Switzerland 37 percent, Japan 31 percent, Spain 27 percent, and the UK [United Kingdom] 23 percent. Turkey plans to build three plants over the next several years. South Korea has eight more reactors coming, Japan 13, China at least 20. France, where nukes generate more than three-quarters of the country's electricity, is privatizing a third of its state-owned nuclear energy group, Areva, to deal with the rush of new business.

The last US nuke plant to be built was ordered in 1973, yet nuclear power is growing here as well. With clever engineering and smart management, nukes have steadily increased their share of generating capacity in the US. The 103 reactors operating in the US pump out electricity at more than 90 percent of capacity, up from 60 percent when Three Mile Island made headlines. That increase is the equivalent of adding 40 new reactors, without bothering anyone's backyard or spewing any more carbon into the air.

So atomic power is less expensive than it used to be—but could it possibly be cost-effective? Even before Three Mile Island sank, the US nuclear industry was foundering on the shoals of economics. Regulatory delays and billion-dollar construction-cost overruns turned the business into a financial nightmare. But increasing experience and efficiency gains have changed all that. Current operating costs are the lowest ever—1.82 cents per kilowatt-hour versus 2.13 cents for coal-fired plants and 3.69 cents for natural gas. The ultimate vindication of nuclear economics is playing out in the stock market: [From 2000 to 2004], the stocks of leading nuclear generating companies such as Exelon and Entergy have more than doubled. Indeed, Exelon is feeling so flush that it bought New Jersey's Public Service Enterprise Group in December [2004], adding four reactors to its former roster of 17.

This remarkable success suggests that nuclear energy realistically could replace coal in the US without a cost increase and ultimately lead the way to a clean, green future. The trick is to start building nuke plants and keep building them at a furious pace. Anything less leaves carbon in the climatic driver's seat. . . .

Taking Nuclear Power Seriously

The more seriously you take the idea of global warming, the more seriously you have to take nuclear power. Clean coal, solar-powered roof tiles, wind farms in North Dakota—they're all pie in the emissions-free sky. Sure, give them a shot. But zero-carbon reactors are here and now. We know we can build them. Their price tag is no mystery. They fit into the existing electric grid without a hitch. Flannel-shirted environmentalists who fight these realities run the risk of ending up with as much soot on their hands as the slickest coal-mining CEO.

America's voracious energy appetite doesn't have to be a bug—it can be a feature. Shanghai, Seoul, and Säo Paolo are more likely to look to Los Angeles or Houston as a model than to some solar-powered idyll. Energy technology is no different than any other; innovation can change all the roles. But if the best we can offer the developing world is bromides about energy independence, we'll deserve the carbon-choked nightmare of a planet we get.

Nuclear energy is the big bang still reverberating. It's the power to light a city in a lump the size of a soda can. Peter Huber and Mark Mills have written an iconoclastic new book on energy, *The Bottomless Well*. They see nuclear power as merely the latest in a series of technologies that will gradually eliminate our need to carve up huge swaths of the planet. "Energy isn't the problem. Energy is the solution," they write. "Energy begets more energy. The more of it we capture and put to use, the more readily we will capture still more."

The best way to avoid running out of fossil fuels is to switch to something better. The Stone Age famously did not end for lack of stones, and neither should we wait for the last chunk of anthracite to flicker out before we kiss hydrocarbons good-bye. Especially not when something cleaner, safer, more efficient, and more abundant is ready to roll. It's time to get real.

"Nuclear power is not the silver bullet for 'solving' the global warming problem."

Nuclear Power Is an Environmentally Unsound Way to Reduce Pollution

Union of Concerned Scientists

Although global warming poses a serious threat, expanding the use of nuclear power is not the answer, claims the Union of Concerned Scientists (UCS) in the following viewpoint. In fact, UCS maintains, the use of nuclear power increases the likelihood of more serious problems. For example, UCS argues, the use of nuclear power could lead to a massive release of radiation or to the theft of nuclear material by terrorists. Indeed, UCS asserts, the Nuclear Regulatory Commission has failed to ensure the safety and security of nuclear plants. UCS is a nonprofit research and activist organization that promotes a healthy environment and a safer world.

As you read, consider the following questions:

1. In the opinion of UCS, why has the nuclear power industry been unable to attract investors?

Union of Concerned Scientists, "Nuclear Power and Global Warming," *Union of Concerned Scientists: Position Paper*, March 2007, pp. 1–4. Copyright © 2007 Union of Concerned Scientists. Reproduced by permission.

2. According to UCS, how should spent nuclear fuel be disposed of?

3. In the author's view, why has the Global Nuclear Energy Partnership failed to solve the nuclear fuel and disposal problems?

Global warming poses a profound threat to humanity and the natural world, and is one of the most serious challenges humankind has ever faced. We are obligated by our fundamental responsibility to future generations and our shared role as stewards of this planet to confront climate change in an effective and timely manner.

The atmospheric concentration of carbon dioxide (the heat-trapping gas primarily responsible for global warming) has reached levels the planet has not experienced for hundreds of thousands of years, and the global mean temperature has risen steadily for over a century as a result. The U.S. National Academy of Sciences, the Intergovernmental Panel on Climate Change, and scientific academies of 10 leading nations have all stated that human activity, especially the burning of fossil fuels, is a major driver of this warming trend. The window for holding global warming emissions to reasonably safe levels is closing quickly. Recent studies have concluded that avoiding dangerous climate change will require the United States and other industrialized countries to reduce their global warming emissions to approximately 20 percent of current levels by mid-century.

What Can Be Done

A profound transformation of the ways in which we generate and consume energy must begin now. The urgency of this situation demands that we be willing to consider all possible options for coping with climate change, but in examining each option we must take into account its impact on public health, safety, and security, the time required for large-scale deployment, and its costs.

While there are currently some global warming emissions associated with the nuclear fuel cycle and plant construction, when nuclear plants operate they do not produce carbon dioxide. This fact is used to support proposals for a large-scale expansion of nuclear power both in the United States and around the world. The Union of Concerned Scientists (UCS) has monitored the use of nuclear power in this country for over three decades, and has been deeply engaged in the related issues of nuclear weapons and proliferation. UCS recognizes the need for a fresh examination of all possible options for coping with climate change, but it must be borne in mind that a large-scale expansion of nuclear power in the United States or worldwide under existing conditions would be accompanied by an increased risk of catastrophic events—a risk not associated with any of the non-nuclear means for reducing global warming.

These catastrophic events include a massive release of radiation due to a power plant meltdown or terrorist attack, or the death of tens of thousands due to the detonation of a nuclear weapon made with materials obtained from a civilian—most likely non-U.S.—nuclear power system. Expansion of nuclear power would also produce large amounts of radioactive waste that would pose a serious hazard as long as there remain no facilities for safe long-term disposal.

Reasons Not to Expand Nuclear Power

In this context, the Union of Concerned Scientists contends that:

1. Prudence dictates that we develop as many options to reduce global warming emissions as possible, and begin by deploying those that achieve the largest reductions most quickly and with the lowest costs and risk. Nuclear power today does not meet these criteria.

2. Nuclear power is not the silver bullet for "solving" the global warming problem. Many other technologies will

be needed to address global warming even if a major expansion of nuclear power were to occur.

3. A major expansion of nuclear power in the United States is not feasible in the near term. Even under an ambitious deployment scenario, new plants could not make a substantial contribution to reducing U.S. global warming emissions for at least two decades.

4. Until long-standing problems regarding the security of nuclear plants—from accidents and acts of terrorism—are fixed, the potential of nuclear power to play a significant role in addressing global warming will be held hostage to the industry's worst performers.

5. An expansion of nuclear power under effective regulations and an appropriate level of oversight should be considered as a longer-term option if other climate-neutral means for producing electricity prove inadequate. Nuclear energy research and development (R&D) should therefore continue, with a focus on enhancing safety, security, and waste disposal.

The Problems with U.S. Nuclear Power Today

Nuclear power currently provides eight percent of the nation's total energy supply, and is now used only to generate electricity. To address global warming we have to address all sources of emissions including transportation.

Since its birth, the nuclear power industry has benefited from major government subsidies. Nevertheless, no new nuclear plants have been ordered since 1978, primarily because the industry has been unable to attract investors after cost overruns and large financial losses.

The Nuclear Regulatory Commission (NRC) has not properly enforced safety regulations at existing plants; such negligence nearly led in 2002 to a catastrophic accident at the Davis-Besse plant in Ohio. Furthermore, NRC security re-

A Chorus of Opponents

Even as debate churns in the newspapers, there is a striking amount of unanimity among the leading environmental organizations that nuclear power does not represent a smart way to address climate change. The National Wildlife Federation, the Union of Concerned Scientists, and the Natural Resources Defense Council (NRDC) are among the many groups arguing there are quicker and cheaper ways to reduce greenhouse gases. What the industry heralds as a "revival," these groups dub a "relapse."

Jason Mark, "The Fission Division: Will Nuclear Power Split the Green Movement," Earth Island Journal, *Autumn 2007.*

quirements still assume that terrorists targeting a nuclear facility will not use aircraft, will not attack with more than a handful of individuals, and will not use widely available weapons such as rocket-propelled grenades.

The disposal of spent nuclear fuel also remains an unresolved issue. Spent fuel rods can, however, be stored safely in aboveground steel cylinders ("dry casks") for at least 50 years. Permanent storage should be in deep underground "geological" sites, but the Yucca Mountain geological facility in Nevada may never be licensed.

Compounding matters is the fact that no new nuclear plants could be completed before 2014 according to government estimates, and plants with genuinely advanced designs no earlier than 2025.

The Appropriate Strategies

A truly effective and timely response to the risk posed by global warming would take the form of a comprehensive national policy covering the entire spectrum of technologies and practices that could reduce global warming emissions. The following strategies would set the nation on a cost-effective and prudent path toward that end:

- The government should adopt policies that maximize energy efficiency and conservation, increase the use of renewable energy resources, and eliminate barriers to existing technologies that can reduce global warming emissions without the risks associated with nuclear power. Such policies provide the best prospect for the large near-term reductions in global warming emissions that are needed to stabilize the global average temperature at a reasonably safe level.

- The government should create conditions under which energy prices would reflect the full cost of global warming emissions, by setting emission targets and establishing a mandatory revenue-neutral carbon tax or cap-and-trade system. A constraint on carbon will make nuclear power more competitive with fossil fuels; how well it would then compete with other technologies that do not generate global warming emissions remains to be seen. Of course, nuclear power's safety, security, nuclear terrorism, and waste problems would still need to be addressed for it to be an acceptable option for reducing global warming emissions.

- Nuclear power should not receive the disproportionate direct and indirect subsidies currently provided by the [George W.] Bush administration and Congress. Start-up subsidies, licensing shortcuts, and liability limits made available through the Price-Anderson Act (which shift financial risk from investors to taxpayers and customers) should not be provided for new nuclear plants.

- Government and industry should recognize that an expansion of nuclear power is contingent on public confidence, and taking shortcuts in either safety or security measures increases the chance of catastrophic events. A serious accident or successful terrorist attack would hobble expansion, as did the accidents at Three Mile Island and Chernobyl, or might even result in the closure of many existing plants.

- Because Yucca Mountain may not be licensed, preliminary assessment of other geological sites should begin. The federal government should take possession of spent fuel (at least at decommissioned reactor sites) and upgrade security of on-site storage. Centralized dry-cask storage should be investigated.

- The government's current investment in energy R&D is less than half its 1979 level, and is minuscule compared with its investment in defense and homeland security R&D. The nation's energy R&D effort should be raised to a level commensurate with the threat to national security posed by global warming.

The Changes Needed

Whether or not there is a major expansion of nuclear power in the United States, the following measures are long overdue, and should be considered prerequisites to any expansion:

- Thorough reform of the NRC; for example, public access to NRC proceedings should be restored to the level that prevailed when nuclear plants were last being licensed.

- Realistic definition of the terrorist threat facing nuclear power plants, and rigorous testing of their readiness for an attack.

- Unambiguous definition of the government's and plant owners' responsibilities for defense against terrorism and sabotage.

Congress should exercise close oversight of the NRC and of the practices employed by the government and industry to protect nuclear plants against terrorism.

The Weapons Implications

A major global expansion of nuclear power would require the United States to adopt domestic and foreign policies that deal effectively with the potential threats to national and global security that would result. Under the existing non-proliferation regime, such an expansion would be irresponsible because it would entail a corresponding growth in facilities for producing nuclear fuels—facilities that can readily produce the materials needed to build nuclear weapons.

The government should, therefore, commit itself to reinforcing the non-proliferation regime so that it can provide reliable control over nuclear fuels.

A nuclear fuel of paramount concern is plutonium, which can serve as a highly effective material for nuclear weapons. For that reason, U.S. policy has long barred the extraction ("reprocessing") of plutonium from spent power reactor fuel. The [George W.] Bush administration broke with this policy by proposing the Global Nuclear Energy Partnership (GNEP), which includes reprocessing as its central component.

Contrary to the administration's claims, GNEP shows no prospect of creating a proliferation-resistant nuclear fuel cycle or of solving the waste disposal problem. The technologies required for turning this vision into reality do not exist, while the proposed waste disposal scheme is considerably more costly and substantially less proliferation-resistant than the current practice of direct disposal of spent fuel. Furthermore, the administration's high-profile advocacy of reprocessing as an integral part of GNEP is encouraging other nations to engage in dangerous plutonium fuel operations.

Congress should therefore restore the U.S. commitment to direct disposal of spent reactor fuel and bar reprocessing. Any congressional commitment to GNEP should await a favorable outcome of a thorough and independent assessment of the program's prospects for success and its implications for national security.

A Lasting Legacy

How we address global warming will be the lasting legacy of this generation. The enormity of the challenge demands that no option for reducing global warming emissions be left permanently off the table. However, the most sensible strategy is to first deploy those options that achieve the largest reductions most quickly and with the lowest costs and risk. As this [viewpoint] has demonstrated, nuclear power today does not meet these criteria.

A major expansion of nuclear power in the United States is not feasible in the near term. Even under an ambitious deployment scenario, new plants could not make a substantial contribution to reducing U.S. global warming emissions for at least two decades.

Long-standing problems regarding the security of nuclear plants must be adequately addressed. A single major accident or successful act of terrorism would likely stop any industry expansion, and could even lead to a contraction that would undermine efforts to address global warming.

The administration's Global Nuclear Energy Partnership (GNEP), which includes extraction of plutonium from spent reactor fuel ("reprocessing") as its central component, shows no prospect of creating a proliferation-resistant nuclear fuel cycle and is encouraging other nations to engage in dangerous plutonium fuel operations. Congress should therefore restore the long-standing U.S. policy barring reprocessing.

An expansion of U.S. nuclear power—under effective regulations and an appropriate level of oversight—should be considered as a longer-term option if other climate-neutral means for producing electricity prove inadequate. Nuclear energy R&D should therefore continue, with a focus on enhancing safety, security, and waste disposal.

> *"Set a firm, economy-wide cap on car-*
> *bon dioxide and other greenhouse gases*
> *. . . to avert the catastrophic conse-*
> *quences of global warming."*

An Emissions Cap and Trading System Will Reduce Global Warming

Environmental Defense

An emissions cap and trade system is the most effective way to reduce global warming, argues Environmental Defense in the following viewpoint. Businesses are motivated to reduce greenhouse gas emissions in a marketplace where they can freely trade credits, the author claims. Companies that develop technologies to reduce emissions can sell credits to those who are unable to do so, the author maintains. Thus, the author reasons, a cap and trade system motivates businesses to come up with efficient technologies to reduce the emissions that contribute to global warming. Environmental Defense promotes market-driven solutions to environmental concerns.

As you read, consider the following questions:

1. What goal does Environmental Defense hope to achieve by 2050?

2. What environmental problem did the author's 1990 cap and trade system successfully combat?

3. According to the author, what state first set comprehensive limits on greenhouse gas emissions?

No longer is global warming some vague problem of the future. It's already damaging our planet at an alarming pace. The Intergovernmental Panel on Climate Change says the evidence is "unequivocal" and concludes that human activities like the burning of fossil fuels have almost certainly caused most of the warming of the past 50 years, bringing extreme weather, stronger storms and more frequent droughts.

Leading scientific organizations around the world, including the U.S. National Academy of Sciences, agree we must act now to slow, stop and reverse the growth of greenhouse gas emissions or face irreversible consequences. Environmental Defense is enlisting influential groups like businesses, farmers and state and local officials to support a national cap on emissions—and working internationally to win needed reductions in developing countries as well. Every piece of this interlocking strategy is needed to solve the puzzle.

The National Climate Campaign

Smart policies, American ingenuity and technologies available today can make the United States a leader in addressing global warming. The Environmental Defense goal is to reduce greenhouse gas emissions 80% by the year 2050 by taking direct aim at the problem. We want to:

- Enact a national cap on greenhouse gas emissions . . . that covers all sectors of the economy.

- Develop and implement a low-carbon fuel standard.

We will achieve these goals through a number of campaigns—from work on biofuels, to legal actions against polluters, to business partnerships with America's top corporations—and we will also work with China, India and rainforest nations to reduce their global warming emissions.

The key is for Congress to pass national legislation that uses a "cap and trade" approach: a strict cap on emissions, coupled with a flexible market-based trading system to reduce emissions at lowest cost.

Our national climate campaign is now ratcheting up the pressure on Congress. To both cut pollution and launch a booming new industry in clean technology, legislation must:

- Set a firm, economy-wide cap on carbon dioxide and other greenhouse gases at levels low enough to avert the catastrophic consequences of global warming.

- Create a carbon marketplace where businesses that reduce emissions more than required earn credits they can sell to others who haven't reduced enough.

- Let the marketplace identify the most innovative and cost-effective technologies to reduce greenhouse gas emissions.

The Key to Success

A cap and trade system insures that reductions actually happen, keeps compliance costs down and lets market forces—rather than the government—pick the best green technologies for each company.

In 1990, when Environmental Defense developed cap and trade and helped put it in place to combat acid rain, *The Economist* called the results "the greatest green success story of the past decade." The same approach will work for global warming.

The technologies to reduce greenhouse gas emissions already exist. . . .

Environmental Defense is building a roster of influential businesses to support our goals. We helped launch the U.S. Climate Action Partnership (USCAP), an unprecedented coalition of top U.S. corporations that have jointly called for an aggressive cap on carbon pollution. Coalition members include Alcoa, BP [British Petroleum], DuPont, GE [General Electric] and PG&E [Pacific Gas and Electric Company].

USCAP maintains that with a coordinated, economy-wide approach, we can cut global warming gases without suffering economic harm.

As Europe and Asia move forward on climate change, America risks losing out on a highly profitable wave of technological development. Our actions today will determine whether the patents on the next generation of clean technology are Chinese, European or American.

Creating Carbon Farmers

More than half of the U.S. is covered by farms, ranches and privately owned forests. Landowners can play an important role in reducing heat-trapping gases. To enlist help from the heartland, Environmental Defense is working to create a new agricultural commodity: greenhouse gas reduction credits. These credits would reward farmers for reducing carbon in the atmosphere. Here's how:

- No-till farming stores carbon in the soil. Limiting nitrogen fertilizers can reduce emissions of nitrous oxide, a potent greenhouse gas.

- Planting forests and restoring wetlands absorbs carbon dioxide and also yields multiple benefits for water and wildlife.

- Small scale, methane capture systems and biofuel refineries reduce transportation and energy costs and cut global warming pollution.

How Cap and Trade Works

A cap and trade system limits the amount of carbon emissions (the cap) and allows clean technology users to sell their carbon credits to businesses that do not meet their targets (the trade).

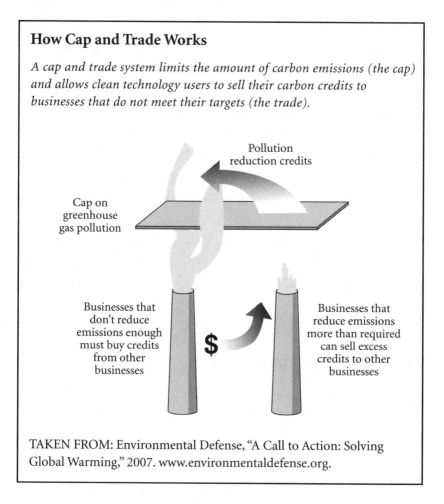

Pollution reduction credits

Cap on greenhouse gas pollution

Businesses that don't reduce emissions enough must buy credits from other businesses

$

Businesses that reduce emissions more than required can sell excess credits to other businesses

TAKEN FROM: Environmental Defense, "A Call to Action: Solving Global Warming," 2007. www.environmentaldefense.org.

Shifting from fossil fuels to plant-based biofuels can lead to dramatic reductions in greenhouse gas emissions. But not all biofuels are created equal. For instance, making ethanol from corn can require large amounts of energy, water and fertilizer and may yield only small net reductions in emissions. How corn is grown and how it is refined can improve the ratio.

Larger gains are achieved by converting the cellulose from agricultural waste, wood chips and fast-growing grasses, such as switchgrass, into fuel. Environmental Defense is working with commodities groups and farmers to develop standards for the best low-carbon fuels.

Seizing the Opportunity

In 2006, California became the first state to set comprehensive limits on greenhouse gas emissions. Environmental Defense co-authored the California law and is helping implement it. We believe the road to national climate action is now being paved by progressive states. That's why we've helped shape two regional cap and trade networks on the East and West coasts, with more networks to come.

Old-fashioned, polluting coal plants are a bad investment. Two top equity firms made that clear in [February 2007]—$45 billion clear—when they bid to buy out Texas energy giant TXU [Texas Utilities]. The deal, which Environmental Defense helped broker, will yield significant benefits for the environment.

But despite the new owners' promise to abandon plans to build eight antiquated coal-fired power plants, the fight is not over. Dozens of dirty coal plants are still on the drawing boards around the nation, threatening to undo climate gains in other sectors. Legal action needs to be taken against delinquent polluters. Cleaner coal plants that capture and dispose of carbon emissions, coupled with a strong energy efficiency program, can meet America's power needs without jeopardizing the environment and human health.

As the debate about global warming shifts from science to economics, we must continue to develop market-based strategies to reduce greenhouse gas emissions, both at home and abroad. Around the world, there is a growing realization among scientists, politicians and business leaders that we must act now, before it's too late. The year 2007 can go down as a turning point in the battle to save the planet from global warming.

> "Carbon capitalism is already out of control, delivering big profits while doing little to halt global warming."

Emissions Trading Will Not Significantly Reduce Global Warming

Fred Pearce

Emissions trading does little to reduce the impact of global warming, claims Fred Pearce in the following viewpoint. In cap and trade programs, which Pearce calls carbon capitalism, governments issue permits that limit the emissions companies can emit. Companies that do not exceed these limits can sell their permits to companies that do, he explains. Unfortunately, some companies profit from selling credits for investments that would have occurred anyway, Pearce asserts. Thus, emissions are not actually offset by the trade, Pearce reasons. Pearce is a science writer and journalist who often writes on environmental issues.

As you read, consider the following questions:

1. According to Nicholas Stern, what is "the greatest market failure the world has ever seen"?

2. In Pearce's view, how much did the value of carbon trading deals grow in 2007?

3. What will happen if carbon capitalism becomes distracted from the present role of the carbon cycle, in the author's opinion?

All the high rollers are in town [Monte Carlo], discussing the biggest bet of them all: that capitalism can save the planet and turn a profit at the same time. In a room near the famous old casino, bankers are talking to green technology companies hungry for cash. Just down the road, at a UN [United Nations] Environment Programme (UNEP) meeting, politicians from around the world are deliberating on how best to lure the financiers into staking their cash on a greener future. Welcome to the dynamic new world of carbon capitalism.

On 1 January [2008] the Kyoto protocol's emissions targets came into full force, creating a long-anticipated market in permits to emit greenhouse gases. To service this marketplace a financial infrastructure of bankers and brokers has sprung up—and people are getting rich. "Carbon is a new commodity, a new currency," says Tom Whitehouse of UK [United Kingdom]-based consultancy Carbon International. "I believe a robust carbon market can and will deliver the emissions cuts that will delay and avert climate change."

Growing Skepticism

On the face of it, even as the wider world economy stutters, everything is going swimmingly for carbon capitalism. Yet, inexplicably, the two sides in Monaco rarely spoke. The politicians never came to talk to the money men and the financiers were not involved in the political deliberations. Was this a mere social oversight, or does it point to a bigger problem? Many fear the latter, claiming that carbon capitalism is already out of control, delivering big profits while doing little to halt global warming. They are deeply sceptical of the notion that market forces can fix climate change. "To believe that is to believe in magic," says Tom Burke, a former director of Friends of the Earth in the UK and adviser to several British environment ministers.

There's little doubt that free-market capitalism helped to get us into the mess we're in. As Nicholas Stern, former chief economist at the World Bank, puts it: climate change is "the greatest market failure the world has ever seen". The question now is whether capitalism is able to make amends. Can it provide a mechanism that rewards people for reducing their carbon emissions instead of increasing them? Or will it simply give big polluters a way of dodging their responsibilities?

Carbon Capitalism Basics

The bare bones of carbon capitalism are simple enough. Under the Kyoto protocol, most industrialised nations except the US have agreed to cut their emissions of greenhouse gases over a five-year period from 2008 to 2012. Governments intend to meet the targets partly by capping the emissions of major industrial polluters—electricity generators, aluminium smelters, cement manufacturers, steel makers and the like. These companies are being issued with permits allowing them to emit only so much carbon dioxide [CO_2] each year. The permits are tradeable—for instance, through the European Emissions Trading Scheme. The thinking is that polluters who can cut their emissions most cheaply will more than meet their legally binding targets and end up with permits to spare. They can then sell these unwanted permits to outfits who are finding it costlier. In this way the Kyoto protocol puts a price on emitting CO_2, and a value on reducing it.

There's more to it, though, than rich-world companies trading permits. Many of the cheapest ways of cutting emissions are to be found in the developing world, where industrial processes are often inefficient and polluting. The Kyoto protocol allows companies in the rich world to invest in emissions-cutting projects in developing countries. This will earn them credits known as certified emissions reductions (CERs) which they can use to offset their own emissions, or trade on the open market. The result is that for every tonne of CO_2 or methane or other greenhouse gas they prevent from spewing up a chimney stack in China, somebody can emit a tonne of gas up a stack in Europe.

This system is known as the Clean Development Mechanism (CDM), and by late [2007] the UN had approved more than 1600 projects for CERs. Carbon capitalists have funded wind turbines in India, geothermal energy in central America and methane capture from landfills in Latin America, and sold the CERs on to the highest bidder.

Alongside the CDM is a growing "voluntary" market in unofficial carbon credits. These are mostly earned by small carbon offsetting schemes that have not gone through the UN accreditation process. They are substantially cheaper than official CERs because they cannot be used to offset Kyoto caps on emissions. Nonetheless, they are popular among individuals and companies who want to voluntarily offset their emissions. The biggest market is in the US, where many companies are keen to show they are doing something.

Most of the companies that want to buy carbon credits have no expertise in green energy projects—or indeed in buying and selling financial instruments as esoteric as carbon credits. So middlemen are moving in, closely followed by speculators. Some set up energy projects to earn carbon credits. Others buy these credits and sell them on. Still others buy options on credits not yet generated or which might be awarded by regulatory regimes that don't yet exist—such as the next phase of the European Emissions Trading Scheme, due to start in 2013. These speculators anticipate that rising prices for carbon permits will eventually deliver a juicy profit.

Trading May Distract from the Real Energy Solutions

By allowing the worst polluters to secure huge blocks of wealth, a grandfathered cap and trade carbon market is likely to encourage the status quo and block innovation rather than provide incentives for immediate investment in long-term structural change. No empirical evidence exists that current greenhouse gas trading programs are functioning as transitional solutions toward a carbon-free future. In fact, all of the available evidence suggests the contrary. . . .

Rather than giving environmentally superior technologies such as solar and wind a leg up in the global market, emissions trading may actually discourage the long-term investment aimed at broad structural change that nearly all sides agree must be started immediately. Granting trading allowances to fossil fuel plants actually acts as an additional subsidy to those plants, making renewables, who do not receive the same subsidies, non-competitive in the market.

Transnational Institute,
"Cap and Trade Is Not the Answer:
An Open Letter," January 31, 2007.

The Carbon Brokers

Even ordinary people are getting involved. For example, if you offset your holiday flights with UK company Climate Care, . . . some of your money will have gone into a Chinese wind turbine project. This was set up by a local company, which sold the carbon credits to a broker, which then sold them to Climate Care, which finally sold some of them to you in the form of the offsetting deal.

Carbon trading is catching on in a big way. In 2007, the value of the deals being done doubled to an estimated $60 billion—though because many credits are traded more than once, the value of credits in circulation is considerably less than this. Nonetheless between now and 2012 European companies are expected to buy about $25 billion worth of carbon credits. With this sort of money up for grabs, it is no surprise that what began as a niche market is now attracting major financial institutions such as Morgan Stanley, Credit Suisse and Barclays Capital. Climate Care has just been bought by JP Morgan.

Yet the critical question remains: does this frenetic activity actually keep greenhouse gases out of the atmosphere? There are widespread fears that it does not. One flaw in the CDM in particular is that credits are being claimed for investments that would have happened anyway, without the added stimulus of earning carbon credits. These projects should not qualify for the CDM because they do not create additional emissions reductions. In fact, they actually make matters worse by allowing companies in the rich world to exceed their limits without genuinely offsetting it elsewhere.

Some of the evidence that this sort of thing is happening is alarming. More than one-third of the official CDM projects approved so far are for hydroelectric dams, mostly in China. The rationale is that by building dams rather than coal-fired power stations, the investors are reducing emissions and so are entitled to carbon credits. Maybe so. But International Rivers, an NGO [non-governmental organization] that campaigns against dams, has shown that most of the dams issued with CERs were either completed or already under construction before the application for carbon credits was made—suggesting they were going to be built anyway, without the incentive of carbon credits. For instance, the Xiaogushan dam in Gansu province began construction in 2003. Later it qualified for carbon credits. Once sold, those credits will allow their purchasers, probably in Europe, to pump out some 3 million tonnes of CO_2 that they would not otherwise have been allowed to emit.

Perhaps surprisingly, there is a widespread view among investors and politicians alike that this is perfectly acceptable. Almost any project that cuts emissions is entitled to carbon credits, they argue—even if those investments would have happened anyway. In Monaco, green technologists were keen to show how adept they were at earning CERs, but many also claimed their schemes would be profitable anyway, without the windfall of carbon credits.

Take the case of Canadian company Polaris Geothermal, which is tapping geothermal energy in Nicaragua. Its chief executive, Tom Ogryzlo, said in Monaco that he had sold CERs equivalent to 100,000 tonnes of CO_2, and would soon be selling a million tonnes a year—worth around 20 million [euro] at today's market rates. "Carbon credits could be 10 per cent of our income," he said. But since he also claimed the project had a rate of return on its sales to the Nicaraguan grid of 25 per cent, that would suggest it may be profitable even without the credits. When we put this to the company, it explained that "Polaris needs the carbon credit revenue in order for the project to be economically attractive and viable."

A Faulty Solution

Situations like this are a weakness of the system itself, which presumes that without the CDM nobody would invest in green technology in developing countries. This assumption is false. Over the past 30 years, global CO_2 emissions have grown only half as fast as the world economy, thanks mainly to cleaner energy generation. As economies develop, they almost always start to use energy more efficiently even without any external incentives. So it is almost unavoidable that some of the carbon credits the CDM hands out go towards projects that would have happened anyway. Advocates of schemes like the

CDM counter this with the argument that whatever their flaws, the pursuit of healthy profits in a buoyant carbon market increases investment in climate-saving technologies.

Investment in green technologies is certainly on the increase. "Mainstream money is flowing into clean tech," says Paul Clement-Hunt, head of UNEP's Finance Initiative. "That is a big market signal. Corporations are building climate change into the way they do business." The London-based consultancy New Energy Finance estimates that $148 billion was invested in renewable energy in 2007, 60 per cent up on 2006. Highlights included wind and solar power, biofuels and the development of lithium-ion batteries, which are expected to be powering new fleets of hybrid cars and buses by 2010.

Even so, critics point out that another reason for the growth of investment in renewable energy is the soaring cost of oil, which has also triggered other developments that are far from climate-friendly—in particular, a rush to exploit dirtier fossil fuels such as coal and tar sands.

The danger now is that governments are seduced into believing the initial success of the carbon market allows them to avoid hard political choices on climate change. But markets are unpredictable, says Burke, and can only be part of the solution if regulated by laws such as a ban on new coal-fired power stations and guaranteed prices for renewable electricity. In other words, the politicians need to go to the casino and cut a deal with the money men.

Another danger of making a market in carbon emissions is the least discussed, but perhaps the most important: only a minority of emissions are covered by legal caps. Most industrial and transport emissions in developing countries remain outside the market. So too do most of the huge emissions caused by deforestation, draining wetlands and ploughing fields.

Displacing the Problem

What that means is that market solutions to carbon emissions risk displacing the problem to activities and places where nobody is counting, and there are no penalties. Most obviously, companies facing limits at home can simply relocate their polluting processes to developing countries where there are no emissions targets. The steel and aluminium industries are already doing this. In November 2007, Ian Rodgers, director of the trade association UK Steel, warned that European carbon pricing "is not going to curb emissions. It will just move the emissions elsewhere".

Just as insidiously, it now makes market sense to cut your emissions in ways that cause much larger emissions from natural ecosystems. You can gain carbon credits for burning biofuels in Europe, even if the crops from which they are produced are grown in fields created by draining peat swamps or cutting down forests. For some hydroelectric schemes, gains are more than outweighed by the methane bubbling up from vegetation rotting in the reservoirs behind the dams.

One answer might be "full carbon accounting", in which all exchanges of greenhouse gases—both into and out of the atmosphere—would have to be included in national and corporate carbon accounts. Remote sensing may soon make this possible.

The danger for now is that carbon capitalism becomes disconnected from the reality of the planet's carbon cycle. If that happens, we face an environmental version of the Enron saga. The giant Texan energy corporation prospered through the 1990s by keeping many of its transactions "off the books". The company appeared wealthy while hiding a mountain of debt. Eventually, someone blew the whistle and the company collapsed. The same thing could happen with carbon capitalism, if big reductions in carbon emissions continue to appear on the books while increases always stay off them.

With Enron, it was the shareholders who suffered. But if the atmosphere continues to be filled with greenhouse gases and the planet's climate crashes as Enron did, no one will be spared.

Periodical Bibliography

The following articles have been selected to supplement the diverse views presented in this chapter.

Drake Bennett — "Emission Control," *Boston Globe*, December 18, 2005.

Marcia Clemmitt — "Climate Change," *CQ Researcher*, January 27, 2006.

Ed Hiserodt — "A Tale of Two Reactors," *New American*, July 7, 2007.

Don Kopecky — "The Limits to Renewable Energy," *Energy Pulse*, May 2, 2008.

Jason Mark — "The Fission Division: Will Nuclear Power Split the Green Movement," *Earth Island Journal*, Autumn 2007.

Patrick McCully — "Kyoto's Great Carbon Offset Swindle," *Renewable Energy World*, June 9, 2008.

Chris Mooney — "The Right Chemistry: Green Chemistry Offers Industry a Way to Reduce Regulatory and Clean-Up Costs with the Proverbial Ounce of Prevention," *American Prospect*, April 2006.

William Nichols — "The Trojan War," *American Scholar*, Autumn 2007.

Jack Spencer — "Nuclear Power Critical to Meeting President's Greenhouse Gas Objectives," *WebMemo [Heritage Foundation]*, April 18, 2008.

Transnational Institute — "Cap and Trade Is Not the Answer: An Open Letter," January 31, 2007. www.tni.org.

Bruce Yandle — "A No-Regrets Carbon Reduction Policy," *PERC Reports*, March 2006.

OPPOSING
VIEWPOINTS®
SERIES

CHAPTER 3

Is the Western Lifestyle Bad for the Environment?

Chapter Preface

Western prosperity and consumption go hand in hand, and with consumption comes waste. In fact, each year Americans generate about 250 million tons of household trash—three times the amount produced in 1960. What to do about the vast quantity of waste produced by the Western lifestyle has, over the years, been the subject of rigorous debate. In the 1960s, nearly all U.S. municipal waste was dumped into landfills. By 2006, however, almost half was diverted to other uses, with more than 32 percent recovered for recycling or composting. Indeed, recycling is one of America's most popular environmental activities. Skeptics claim, however, that recycling does little to help the environment and often costs more than burying waste in landfills. Indeed, the recycling debate is reflective of other controversies surrounding the impact of the Western lifestyle on the environment.

Those who support recycling believe that it is an important way to reduce the impact of Western consumption on the environment. "People understand recycling—it's the most widely practiced environmental activity in the U.S.," maintains Allen Hershkowitz, a senior scientist with the Natural Resources Defense Council (NRDC). The goods made from recycling scrap metal, glass, or paper use less energy and therefore generate fewer greenhouse gases than goods created from natural resources, supporters assert. "Recycling is ecologically superior to using virgin materials. When you make aluminum from recycled cans instead of bauxite ore," Hershkowitz claims, "you save 95 percent of the energy." Recycling also is good for the economy, some commentators claim. For example, the scrap-recycling industry generates an estimated $65 billion in revenues annually and employs some 50,000 people. Recycling also combats climate change by reducing the powerful greenhouse gas, methane, which is produced when organic waste decays in landfills, some analysts argue. Recycling also reduces littering and the costs of disposal, making it popular among state and local governments, which are often responsible for solid waste disposal.

Skeptics suggest, however, that recycling is a poor use of resources. For example, critics claim, the recyclable materials found in municipal waste are often of low value and are expensive to reuse or recycle. Unlike glass, plastic typically cannot be processed directly back into its original form, so recylcing often means "downcycling" it into a lesser-quality product. For example, plastic bottles are often made into fleece for jackets. After that, however, the plastic becomes waste. Even several recycling advocates, such as BringRecycling.org, acknowledge that in some cases, recycling is simply "delaying the inevitable union of material and trash heap." Recycling critics also contend that money dedicated to recycling could be better used elsewhere. H. Sterling Burnett, senior fellow at the National Center for Policy Analysis, maintains that Orange County Florida spends approximately $3 million a year to collect recyclables that it sells for only $56,000. In Burnett's view, "this money is no longer available for other worthwhile social goods like new schools, more police, better roads, housing and medical care for the poor and open space for parks." Burnett concludes, "recycling is, undoubtedly, sometimes worthwhile, but as with old clothes and used books, it is probably best to let people rather than governments decide which items are reused and when."

Whether recycling is an effective way to reduce the vast waste produced by the Western lifestyle remains the subject of debate. The authors in the following chapter debate other issues surrounding the controversy over the impact of the Western lifestyle on the environment.

| "The evidence for the impact on global warming of affluent lifestyles is now incontrovertible."

The Western Lifestyle Threatens the Environment and Human Well-being

Kate Soper

Western affluence and consumerism—the idea equating human happiness with material possessions—threatens the environment and human well-being, claims Kate Soper in the following viewpoint. Unfortunately, she argues, placing limits on consumption to protect the environment runs counter to global capitalism. Nevertheless, Soper suggests that people are questioning the value of consumerism not only because of its environmental impact but also because it gets in the way of healthier values. People must abandon the presumption that progress is synonymous with consumption, she reasons. Soper, a British philosopher, often writes about environmental issues.

As you read, consider the following questions:

1. According to Soper, in what ways does disenchantment with the negative by-products of affluence find expression?

Kate Soper, "The Other Pleasures of Post-Consumerism," *Soundings*, Spring 2007, pp. 31–40. Copyright © 2007 Lawrence & Wishart Ltd. Reproduced by permission.

2. To what does information overload contribute, in the author's view?

3. What examples does the author provide of the interconnection among modes of consumption?

The evidence for the impact on global warming of affluent lifestyles is now incontrovertible and receiving belated mainstream media attention. One has to be glad of this. But it is difficult not to be disheartened by the blinkered nature of the two most commonly encountered reactions. On the one hand, there are the carpe diem [seize the day] fatalists. Resigned to the prospect of ecological devastation, they see little point in mending their profligate ways, since the impact globally will be so minimal. Every percentage reduction of carbon emissions in the UK [United Kingdom], they point out, will be more than cancelled out by their increase in China or India. As the counter to this we have the technical-fix optimists, who believe—or hope—that new technologies will solve the problem, thus ensuring continued economic growth with very little alteration in our life-style. Provided we make the investment now, the 'pain', as these optimists put it, can be kept to a minimum.

Promoting Consumerism

I shall not here address the particular arguments of these responses, nor seek to arbitrate between them. What concerns me, rather, is what they share in common, namely, the presumption that the consumerist model of the 'good life' is the one we want to hold on to as far as we can; and that any curb on that will necessarily be unwelcome and distressing. Neither the 'seize the day' fatalists nor the technical optimists dwell on the negative consequences of Euro-American-style affluence for consumers themselves (the stress, ill-health, congestion, pollution, noise, excessive waste); and neither suggest it might be more fun to escape the confines of the growth-driven, shopping-mall culture than to continue to keep it on track. We hear all too little of what might be gained by moving away from our current obsession with consumerist gratifications, and pursuing a less work-driven and acquisitive way of life.

The reason for this is obvious. Counter-consumerism is bad for business. It is ultimately incompatible with the continued flourishing of de-regulated global capitalism. (It is a measure of the Stern report's alienation that it cites the risk to economic growth as the main reason for attempting to curb carbon emissions, when it is, of course, that very growth that is the major factor in their creation.) The market economy, in short, is averse to the promotion of any non-commodified conceptions of human gratification and personal development. Its main productive mission is not human or environmental well-being, but the multiplication and diversification of 'satisfiers' that can realise profit; and since this mission runs entirely counter to any idea of accommodation to natural limits, it can hardly surprise us that alternative conceptions of the good life have been so under-represented in consumer society. Indeed, everything conspires to ensure minimal outlet to any countering imaginary, and the forces arrayed against it are truly formidable. . . .

The Counter-Consumerist Movement

Yet despite this virtual repression of alternatives, there are signs—and *The Good Society*, recently published as part of the Compass programme for renewal is a timely response to these—that the contradictions between capitalist and ecological pressures, and between what the economy demands and what is humanly most valued, will not be contained indefinitely. Shopping may still be one of the nation's favourite ways of spending time, and there has been precious little reform in the use of the car and air flight, yet there is also disenchantment with the negative by-products of the affluent lifestyle, and a growing sense that it may stand in the way of other

© 2008 Andy Singer, and PoliticalCartoons.com.

equally—if not more—valued goals. Such disaffection may find expression in nostalgia for certain kinds of material, or for objects and practices that no longer figure in everyday life; it may lament the loss of certain kinds of landscape, or spaces (to play or talk or loiter or meditate or commune with nature); it may deplore the fact that were it not for the dominance of the car, there would be an altogether different system of provision for other modes of transport, and both rural and city

areas would look and feel and smell and sound entirely different. Or it may just take the form of a vague and rather general malaise that descends in the shopping mall or supermarket: a sense of a world too cluttered and encumbered by
material objects and sunk in waste, of priorities skewed
through the focus on ever more extensive provision and accumulation of things.

Although these kinds of reactions are doubtless driven
partly by an altruistic concern for the global ecological and
social consequences of the consumerist life-style, they are also
distinguished by self-interested motivations. . . .

Clearly individuals who think this way are currently in a
minority. But, arguably, they form the avant garde [the forefront of an action or a movement] of a counter-consumerist
movement and green renaissance that could well gather increasing momentum over the next decades, eventually posing
a more serious threat to the market-driven economy and cultural hegemony of our times. The dependency of globalised
capitalism on the continued preparedness of its consumers to
remain forever unsated—forever fobbed off with compensa-
tory forms of gratification, forever nonchalant about the consequences of consumerism both socially and ecologically—is
now beginning to be recognised, across the political spectrum,
as one of the more significant sources of dialectical tension of
our times. This finds its most explicit expression in the expansion of green and ethical consumption. . . .

The Homogenous Lifestyle

We need therefore to be more assertively utopian in promoting sustainable consumption . . . This involves, in turn, a challenge to contemporary conceptions of 'progress', and a more
historically informed understanding of the regressive aspects
of consumerism. Advocates . . . may also want to question
some of the gains of the age of 'comfort' and 'convenience'.
The machines and lifts and escalators and moving walk-ways

that reduce our energy expenditure do so at the cost of the exertion of muscular power and the sense of vitality that goes along with that. Constant grazing and 'comfort' eating deprives those who 'indulge' in it of the enjoyment of satisfying a sharpened hunger and thirst. And food satiety and over-provisioning create a vast amount of waste. . . . The central heating and air-conditioning that ensures that we are continuously in the 'comfort' zone in homes, offices, airports and shopping malls has certainly cut out the pain of extreme temperatures, but it has also made interior space more boringly homogeneous, and reduced sensitivity to seasonal changes.

What needs challenging above all is the presumption that 'progress' and 'development' are synonymous with speeding up and saving time. Today it is well-nigh impossible to travel long-distance other than by air, and it would be thought grotesque for industrial designers to promote product innovations on the grounds that they allowed their users to proceed at a more relaxed pace. Speed is, of course, convenient—and can be thrilling. Yet there is also a relative dimension to both these attributes, of which we should be aware. Travelling by chaise [carriage] at fifteen miles an hour was regarded as exhilaratingly rapid by Charles Dickens, who in *Pickwick Papers* describes fields, trees and hedges rushing past at that pace 'with the velocity of a whirlwind'. Today a twenty miles per hour speed limit is regarded by car-users as restrictively slow. (There are, in any case, more absolute limits on road capacity and the speeds at which drivers themselves can operate with relative safety.) A comparable dialectic is at work in our capacity to respond to the increasing computing power of silicon chips (which currently doubles every eighteen months). We have certainly very quickly adapted to—and indeed become extraordinarily dependent upon—the fast processing of information and the billions of electronic exchanges this allows on a daily basis. But there is a lot of evidence, too, to suggest that information overload is a major contributor to stress at work, and that the innovations are not always unmitigated blessings.

The Structure of Consumption

But the demand for speed of both transport and communication is relative in a further and rather different respect, since how fast we want—or 'need'—to travel (or communicate) is itself a function of other aspects of an overall life-style and pattern of consumption. Urbanisation goes together with developments such as commuting and loss of rural shops and services, developments that in turn are dependent upon provision of faster means of transport. The affluent modern life-style is a structure of interconnected modes of consumption, each one of which is integral to the whole and reliant upon it. But, for that very reason, shifts in one area will always have knock-on effects in others, and thus influence the overall structure of consumption. Were car use severely restricted, lives would be saved, communities revitalised, and children released from the nervy surveillance of their elders, as well as the dangers posed by adults constantly encroaching on them with their motorised vehicles. Were more people to shop by bike or bus rather than car, it would encourage the return of high street retailers, and fewer small stores would be forced into closing because of parking restrictions in town centres. Were we to reduce the working week or the work loads expected of employees within the working day, it would bring with it a relaxation of the speed at which goods and information were required to be delivered or transmitted. Were airfreight to be curbed, it would have a major impact on the sourcing of perishable goods and significantly reduce the mileage travelled by many articles of everyday consumption—with benefits for consumers, the local economy and the environment.

VIEWPOINT

> "Lifestyle changes that emphasize greater efficiency, less consumption, and genuine personal sacrifice may feel good and make for good press, but they rarely help the earth."

Lifestyle Changes Will Not Improve the Environment

Paul Wapner and John Willoughby

In the following viewpoint, Paul Wapner and John Willoughby assert that lifestyle changes do little if anything to improve the environment. Asking people to reduce consumption, the authors assert, merely diverts savings to others who will use these funds for projects that deplete resources. The environmental harm is simply shifted from one locale to another, Wapner and Willoughby reason. Only by making major changes in the world economy will the environment be effectively improved, they argue. At American University, Wapner is an associate professor and the director of the Global Environmental Politics program, and Willoughby is a professor of Economics.

Paul Wapner and John Willoughby, "The Irony of Environmentalism: The Ecological Futility but Political Necessity of Lifestyle Change," *Ethics & International Affairs*, December 2005, pp. 17–29. Copyright © 2005 Carnegie Council for Ethics in International Affairs. Reproduced by permission.

As you read, consider the following questions:

1. According to Wapner and Willoughby, what has the environmental movement been explaining since its inception?

2. In the authors' opinion, in addition to ecological conditions, what is environmentalism about?

3. Although the choice to have fewer children or fewer things may not directly protect the earth, what can these choices influence, in the authors' view?

Many environmentalists point to overpopulation and over-consumption as the fundamental causes of environmental harm. They argue that there are simply too many human beings, in terms of sheer numbers, and too many of us who overuse the earth's resources (and thus generate significant amounts of waste) to live ecologically sustainable lives. The fundamental tasks of environmentalism, then, are to lower population rates and curtail consumption. These twin objectives have defined much of the environmental movement for decades, and both trajectories course through contemporary environmentalism, urging us all to cut back: to curtail our numbers and our appetites.

Lowering population and curbing consumption are not simply governmental or corporate tasks, but also involve individual lifestyle choices. The decisions we each make in terms of whether to have children and, if so, how many, and what level of material comfort to experience translate into widespread fertility and consumption patterns. As the environmental movement has been explaining since its inception over a century ago, environmental protection entails, as the saying goes, "walking lightly on the earth." And, as the surge of such best-selling books as *Voluntary Simplicity* and *50 Simple Things You Can Do to Save the Earth* explain, this is something we can *all* learn to do.

Questioning Assumptions

While acting at the microlevel to reduce family size and consume less is almost dogma among environmentalists, there are reasons to question their admonitions, or at least to specify the conditions under which such activities would genuinely make a difference in terms of environmental well-being. In this article we argue that prescriptions that call for individually reducing consumption and having fewer children are valid only under highly restricted conditions, conditions that are generally unacknowledged by environmental researchers and activists. In fact, we show that the conditions are so narrow that, for most people most of the time, lifestyle changes are ecologically irrelevant.

Many environmentalists call for reducing family size and consuming less because they see these as ways to decrease the total amount of spending within an economy. Reduced spending limits the demand for resources and the production of waste, and thus contributes to environmental well-being. . . . However, while less spending within an economy may, in fact, minimize environmental harm, it is not the case that cutting back on individual consumption or having a smaller family will reduce overall spending. In most cases, such actions will simply shift the locus of spending. If a family, for example, continues to receive the same amount of income but decides to buy fewer products or have fewer children (and thus forgo the consumption associated with additional family members), they have more savings at their disposal. In fact, much of the literature advocating less consumption and greater consumer simplicity emphasizes the bonus of extra savings. It is crucial to recognize, however, that savings do not simply sit in banks or other financial portfolios; rather, they are deployed by financial institutions to fund investment projects. Consequently, because purchasing power is fungible, it makes little difference ecologically if one saves or invests money rather than spends it. For, aside from placing money under one's mattress, it will

America's Narrow Environmental Imagination

An accelerating individualization of responsibility in the United States is narrowing, in dangerous ways, our "environmental imagination" and undermining our capacity to react effectively to environmental threats to human well-being. Those troubled by overconsumption, consumerism and commodification should not and cannot ignore this narrowing. Confronting the consumption problem demands, after all, the sort of institutional thinking that the individualization of responsibility patently undermines. It calls too for individuals to understand themselves as citizens in a participatory democracy first, working together to change broader policy and larger social institutions, and as consumers second.

*Michael F. Maniates, "Individualization:
Plant a Tree, Buy a Bike, Save the World?"*
Global Environmental Politics, *August 2001.*

most likely be used by investors to create more economic wealth, and this will be done primarily by funding practices that use resources and create waste. . . .

The Limits of Lifestyle Changes

Unless one invests savings in particular, very circumscribed ways, one is not necessarily supporting environmental protection. Money withheld from one sector simply gets channeled into another. To the degree that this is the case, the irony of environmentalism is that the very practices that seemingly hold promise for environmental protection at the individual level become a matter of merely shifting the locale of environmental harm. Lifestyle changes that emphasize greater efficiency, less consumption, and genuine personal sacrifice may feel good and make for good press, but they rarely help the earth.

This argument is troubling and, when we first developed it, it threatened our most cherished assumptions about environmentalism. Both of us believe that environmental problems represent some of the most profound challenges that humanity faces, and that there is an important role for individual choice in environmental politics. But . . . we have come to see the benefits of that choice more in moral terms and for the good of political agency rather than as a direct causal influence on ecological conditions. For many, this may diminish the meaning of individual choice when choosing to reduce consumption or our progeny. . . . However, such a reaction is inappropriate. By circumscribing and analyzing the genuine environmental effects of lifestyle choices, we can better appreciate their influence.

While such influence may be less on bio-physical systems than on political forces, this takes nothing away from the informed actions of individuals. Rather, an accurate understanding of their political influence provides greater hope for environmental protection, because we can focus more rigorously on actions that actually help to protect the earth's ecosystems. . . .

A Need for Broad Economic Changes

Our research shows that the structure of the economy frustrates individuals' efforts to protect the environment by maintaining the fungibility of money and demanding that finances be continually deployed in the service of investment and productivity. In other words, impediments to environmental protection are structural, and environmentalists must consequently embrace a politics that focuses on changing the nature of the world economy, rather than tinkering with individual practices that are fundamentally regulated by the economy itself. . . .

It is important to make one caveat. We do not question the environmentalist insight that people must consume less in the service of environmental protection. The ideal of environmentalism must include, as [ecological economist] Herman Daly, [environmental analyst] Lester Brown, and numerous others point out, reducing the overall amount of raw materials and energy used by a society, or what is often called throughput. Rather, we question the injunction that the best route to less consumption is through individual action. Individual action within the current world economy will not reduce overall throughput, but will simply change where the engines of consumption operate. . . .

Making Responsible Choices

People make at least two choices when they take personal action to limit their impact on the earth, yet many are conscious of only one. Many people throughout the world are choosing to have smaller families and to use fewer resources (and thereby produce less waste) for environmental reasons. These actions should be applauded. Unfortunately, our responsibilities do not end after this choice. We must also choose what to do with the additional money we often possess as a result of our initial choices. As mentioned, one result of not having children or of reducing consumption is the opportunity to spend and save. To see our actions fully through, we must take environmental responsibility for this opportunity. To the degree that our expenditures and savings go into productive processes that use resources and generate waste beyond essential needs, our efforts will not achieve our intended aims. As we have noted, however, taking environmental responsibility to realize such aims is something that cannot be done easily as individuals or rest on personal abilities to track and manage the consequences of our individual choices. Rather, we can be most effectively responsible only within political economic conditions that deliberately reduce throughput. Ushering in such a system must be part of genuine environmentalism.

Having said this, it would be irresponsible of us to end without saying something about the initial choices themselves. Although these choices may fall short of achieving demonstrable environmental protection, they nonetheless stand as important moral and political actions. This should not be lost in the above analysis.

Ethics and Politics

Environmentalism is not simply about the earth's ecological conditions; it is also about the kinds of people we wish to be. One thing often ignored by analysts is the ethical aspirations of environmentalists. As [environmental ethics researcher] Leslie Paul Thiele has explained, environmentalism is essentially about extending one's moral concern across time, space, and species; that is, environmentalists wish to leave a healthy planet to future generations, to protect fellow humans who live "downstream" from experiencing the ill effects of environmental degradation, and to protect the nonhuman world. Behind all of this is a moral sensitivity for others. It represents a sense of concern and solidarity with other people and other living beings. That environmentalists of all stripes work to express this concern politically is one of the most admirable dimensions of environmentalism.

When individuals seek to live the change they wish to bring about, or, put differently, when they prefigure the future they want to create, we should all take note. This is especially the case with environmentalists who sacrifice many personal desires for the well-being of others. Such action, which includes limiting family size and curtailing consumption, represents important moral behavior, and although it may not translate directly into actual biophysical changes in the world, there is no reason to belittle it. If we are ever to create an ecologically sound world in which social structures and individuals operate in ways that enhance environmental well-being, it will be based on, and inspired by, the model of action individual environmentalists undertake in their personal lives. In the context of this article, this means that lifestyle choices can inspire and mobilize people to seek alternative forms of economic activity—specifically ones that do not lead to endless consumption. So, although choosing to have fewer children or fewer things may not directly protect the earth because of the economic trade-offs involved, one should still undertake and support such actions because they can influence economic, social, and political institutions and, at a more basic level, hold the key toward achieving meaningful environmental living.

| "The dumping of e-waste has grown into
| . . . an environmental disaster."

Electronic Waste Hurts the Environment

Ellen Ruppell Shell

Constant innovation has made the shelf life of electronics brief, claims Ellen Ruppell Shell in the following viewpoint. As a result, she argues, people have discarded tons of electronics, such as cell phones, computers, peripherals, and media players, and their toxic contents are left to leak into the environment. In addition, Shell maintains that much of the technology sent to recycling centers ends up in the developing world, where worker safety is less of a priority. She suggests that programs should emulate the safe and successful e-waste recycling that occurs in Switzerland. Shell is a professor of science journalism at Boston University.

As you read, consider the following questions:

1. How many computers became obsolete between 2000 and 2005 in the United States, according to Shell?

2. How many nations does Shell report agreed to ban the export of hazardous waste to less wealthy countries in 1995?

Ellen Ruppell Shell, "Thrashed: Ever Wonder Where the Cell Phone or Computer You Toss Ends Up?" *Audubon*, May/June 2008, pp. 90–97. Copyright © 2008 National Audubon Society. Reproduced by permission.

3. In the author's opinion, why is the "mining" of electronics extremely profitable?

My basement is a mausoleum of sorts, cluttered with memorabilia harking back to childhood. Deep in its depths, behind the sports equipment and long-forgotten board games, lurks a jumble of electronic gadgetry—computers, monitors, and printers—that for me have outlived their usefulness. These are formidable objects, hefty machines that I know, instinctively, do not belong in the trash. So the pile remains, trapped in a twilight zone between desktop and dump, a sorry reminder of the power of Moore's Law.

A Torrent of E-Waste

Gordon Moore, a cofounder of Intel Corporation, famously observed more than 40 years ago that computer processing power doubles every two years, the corollary being that all the machines suddenly rendered half as powerful as the current standard are on an inexorable march toward obsolescence. In the United States alone, an estimated 197 million computers made this trek between 2000 and 2005, according to the International Association of Electronics Recyclers. But computers are only one tributary feeding this torrent of "e-waste." Every year Americans "retire" an estimated 130 million cell phones and untold tons of printers, copiers, keyboards, mice, portable media players, VCRs, scanners, and digital cameras.

While some of this detritus languishes in attics and basements, the U.S. Environmental Protection Agency (EPA) estimates that each year about two million tons of it are dumped and left to fall apart and leak their toxic innards across the landscape. Discarded electronics comprise 70 percent of heavy metal contamination in the nation's landfills, a horrifying thought for anyone who worries about public health. The international prospect is even more daunting, though also hopeful, as I was to observe during my 10,000-mile journey on the e-waste trail through Europe and China. But before I left, I decided to take a look at the problem closer to home.

The dumping of e-waste has grown into such an environmental disaster that I tried to ignore the tangle of computers and printers hiding in the basement, where at least they could do no harm. But when I learned I could unload the stuff safely not far from my home in Newton, Massachusetts, I dutifully excavated an ancient IBM [International Business Machines] desktop and drove it to a nearby "transfer station" for recycling. An attendant pointed me to a room-sized container crammed nearly to the roof with outdated electronics. I wedged my machine among the other castoffs and silently pledged to return the following week with the rest of the electronic junk lurking in my basement. Doing good had never been so easy.

In truth I had no idea where that computer was headed. When I asked Elaine Gentile, director of Newton's Division of Environmental Affairs, she seemed surprised. Apparently not many people concern themselves with the trajectory of their abandoned electronics. Gentile told me my computer was likely en route to the Massachusetts headquarters of CRT Recycling Inc., a company that trucks roughly 20 tons of discarded computers, television sets, and other electronics out of my small city every month.

CRT Recycling is housed in a low-slung, ramshackle building whose entrance seems to be a secret. It took me some time to find the door, and when I did and walked inside it was clear why signage was not a priority—the place was cavernous, cacophonous, strewn with junk, and definitely not for tourists. General manager Peter Kopcych waved me into the relative quiet of his office. A compact yet burly man, he wore a sweatshirt that bore the mark of one too few launderings. Kopcych rose from behind his desk and gathered a small entourage of employees to escort me on a tour.

The Unique Problem of E-Waste

The trouble is that e-waste is unwanted in landfills because of its volume. It has unique environmental problems that might include high lead content in screens, complex and toxic plastics in computers, unsafe alloys in phones and even, in some appliances, microscopic amounts of uranium.

Deborah Cameron,
"Lust for Upgrades Builds a Mountain of e-Waste,"
Sydney Morning Herald, *April 16, 2007.*

Walking deep into the din we came to an open area raucous with salsa music and littered with cardboard boxes the size of Shetland ponies. Kopcych buys these "gaylords" for three bucks apiece from truckers hauling produce from the West Coast. His workers peel out the wilted lettuce leaves, line the boxes with protective plastic, and fill them with wire, gears, plastic parts, printers, keyboards, computers, battery packs, and broken glass from cathode ray tubes. As we chatted a virtual United Nations of recycling entrepreneurs filed by: A two-man team rummaged a hillock of computer printers, yanking out the ink cartridges to refill at their Rhode Island factory and sell on the secondhand market. A pair of Haitian dealers combed through a pile of television sets, culling the best ones for sale in their home country. A couple of guys from the Dominican Republic clipped compressors from a lineup of rusting refrigerators. This was low-hanging fruit, parts that can be readily refurbished and resold at a profit. But the bulk of Kopcych's booty gets shipped to the developing world.

The Export of Hazardous E-Waste

[In 1995,] more than 62 nations agreed to a ban on the export of hazardous waste—including electronic waste—from wealthy to less wealthy countries. Since then several more countries have signed on, but some major players—Canada, Australia, and the United States among them—have not ratified the ban, and it does not yet wield the force of law. This foot-dragging, environmentalists complain, has stalled reform. "Free and easy export of waste to the developing world is killing incentives for American recyclers to do the right thing," says Jim Puckett, coordinator of the Basel Action Network, an environmental advocacy group. "Americans are less willing to invest in change because it's so cheap to simply ship waste abroad and so profitable to poison the poor."

Kopcych insists he is poisoning no one. For example, he says, he used to ship glass yanked from cathode ray tubes (CRTs) by workers wearing face masks and Kevlar gloves to "a beautiful facility" in Brazil, where a factory recycled it into new CRTs for the South American market. Now he sends it to facilities in Malaysia or India. More than half the weight of a CRT is in two layers of glass, one coated with barium oxide, melted in, one with lead. Barium oxide is an irritant to lungs and skin; lead, a deadly neurotoxin. No one wants either poison leaching into the soil or—worse—the groundwater, and in 2000 Massachusetts became the first state to ban CRTs from landfills. California and then seven other states have since followed suit. In these states, CRTs must either be reused or dismantled, their component parts often dealt with individually or disposed of outside of the state's borders.

So reuse sounds like a good option. But environmentalists worry about passing off leaded glass to the developing world, where it could leach into the soil or water supply. They worry, too, about all the other bits Kopcych and his fellow recyclers ship to parts of the world where face masks and Kevlar gloves are in short supply. Electronics contain exotic metals, many of them toxic to humans. In addition, the mining of these metals has wreaked havoc and despair across the landscapes of many countries. "Forty-five percent of all toxics produced by industry in the U.S. comes from mining," says Robin Ingenthron, founder of Good Point, a recycling company in Vermont. "And it's even worse in some other countries." A few years ago the mining of coltan, an essential ingredient in cell phones, was linked to the slaughter of eastern gorillas in the Congo. In the country's Kahuzi Biega National Park, the gorilla population was cut to nearly a quarter of what it was 14 years ago as miners deforested the land, rebels occupied the area, and hunters targeted the animals that survived as bush meat. Though the coltan rush has abated for now (thanks to a decline in price), mining could still pose a serious threat to the region's wildlife.

Mining Electronics

Electronics recycling can reduce this problem, as valuable minerals, instead of being wrenched out of the ground, are extracted from old machines and reused. Such "mining" of electronics can be extremely profitable: Each ton of cell phones contains more than 12 ounces of gold, nearly 8 pounds of silver, and 286 pounds of copper. Circuit boards contain more gold by volume than does gold ore. Smelters in Europe and Canada can melt components at super-high temperatures to extract lead, copper, and other elements. These facilities are held to strict environmental and health standards, and the one I visited in Belgium, Umicore Precision Metal Refining, is an efficient and well-run place. The company, the world's largest precious metal recycler, extracts silver, gold, and 15 other metals from tons of cell phones, circuit boards, and other abandoned electronics. "It's an environmental challenge but also a resource opportunity," a Umicore scientist told me. "Smelting electronics reduces the need for mining, reduces the risk of toxic metals leaking into the environment, and is also good business."

Unfortunately, only five such smelters exist in the world for e-scrap, none of them in the United States, and their services do not come cheap. Which helps explain why roughly 80 percent of "recycled" electronics in this country are shipped to poor nations with lackluster or poorly enforced environmental and health regulations.

Electronic waste harbors roughly half of all the elements on the periodic table, from arsenic to zinc. Left unchecked, these toxins can cause enormous damage, especially in poor countries with no or little environmental remediation. The dumping of electronic trash is proliferating badly in Korea, Indonesia, Vietnam, Africa, India, Bangladesh, and especially China.

China is ravenous for raw materials, and there are hundreds of thousands of hands there willing and able to mine metal and plastic from the detritus of wealthier nations. The country technically banned the importation of electronic waste in 2002, but a [2007] trip to the booming port city of Taizhou, about 150 miles south of Shanghai, gave ample evidence that the ban lacks teeth. . . .

Successful E-Waste Recycling

Sadly, what some call the "effluence of our affluence" is endangering those who can least protect themselves. But this need not be the case. As the people of Switzerland have amply demonstrated, littering the world with our castoffs is not only unethical; in an era of quickly depleting resources, it is unwise.

Switzerland is a small country with few mineral resources and a scarcity of land. Landfills here are not an option. This helps explain why in 1991 Switzerland became the first country in Europe—and the world—to implement a federally regulated e-waste recycling program. . . .

In Switzerland 98 percent of electronic waste is recycled or incinerated to produce energy in clean-burning factories fitted with scrubbers to prevent air pollution. In St. Galen alone this energy heats 10,000 homes. Peter Bomand, former chairman of the Environmental Commission of the Swiss Association for Information, Communication and Organizational Technology, told me that the Swiss have always been conscious of their trash, and their natural resources. "We are a small country with no access to the sea and no raw materials," he said. "The problem in the United States is that you believe your resources are endless."

In the European Union, waste from electric and electronic equipment (or WEEE) accounts for roughly eight percent of all waste on the continent. But the ELI [Environmental Law Institute] is addressing the problem with legislation that bans certain toxics from electronics, and an initiative that requires electronics manufacturers to take back from consumers their used and outdated equipment and dispose of it in a responsible manner. The WEEE Initiative didn't take hold until January 2007, but several European countries began taking steps to deal with electronic waste long before this.

In a global economy hungry for natural resources, it has become increasingly clear that recycling is more energy efficient, safer, and more economical than many of its alternatives, especially mining. In the United States, a budding awareness of the inherent value of electronic components has contributed to the explosive growth in electronics recycling. Cell phones—which contain about 60 cents' worth of precious metal each—can now be "bought back," or traded in for new phones, though this is not yet a common practice. And concerns with computer security and the environment have caused some businesses to insist that their discarded machines not leave the country, or end up in a landfill. In the United States there are as yet no national laws or regulations concerning the recycling or shipping of electronics, but a handful of states—California, Maine, Maryland, Massachusetts, Minnesota, New Jersey, North Carolina, Texas, Oregon, and Washington—have instituted controls, such as forcing producers to take back computers and other electronics for recycling. It's likely that more states and more regulations will follow.

America and the world have a longstanding love affair with technology, and few of us can resist the latest gadgets. Thanks to tireless innovation, the shelf life of electronics is brief—the average cell phone is discarded or traded in after about 18 months. Perhaps it's time to awaken to the ugly side of our high-tech habits.

Obviously much work remains to be done. Returning home from Switzerland, I saw that Pizza Hut was offering a free cell phone with the purchase of a large pie. Based on what I had seen in China, I knew that those cell phones were anything but free.

| "There is no scientific evidence that substances from e-waste present a discernable risk to human health or the environment."

The Problem of Electronic Waste Is Exaggerated

Dana Joel Gattuso

Claims that electronic waste poses a serious threat to the environment are exaggerated, maintains Dana Joel Gattuso in the following viewpoint. E-waste, she argues, comprises only a small percentage of U.S. waste. Moreover, Gattuso asserts, evidence shows that substances leaking from e-waste pose no risk to public health. Those who abhor the shipping of e-waste to the developing world can blame the rush to mandate recycling, she suggests. Recyclers send e-waste to these nations because recycling is much cheaper there, she concludes. Gattuso is a policy analyst with the Competitive Enterprise Institute, a libertarian think tank.

As you read, consider the following questions:

1. Where do most home computers in the United States end up, in Gattuso's estimation?

2. According to the author, what percentage of the 1999 total municipal solid waste stream did e-waste constitute?

3. In the author's opinion, what reactions did the report *Exporting Harm: The High-Tech Trashing of Asia* inspire?

In the home, computers are becoming as commonplace as toasters. Rapid improvements in technology and design, as well as increased competition, have made home computers more affordable than ever. Only 14 years ago, 16 percent of U.S. households owned a home computer; today, more than half own at least one computer.

The Home Computer Revolution

Innovation and affordability have also enabled computer manufacturers to roll out new, faster, and upgraded models at a prodigious rate. Since 1981, more than a billion personal computers have been sold worldwide—400 million of those in the United States. In 2003 alone, more than 50 million computers were sold in the U.S.

A natural byproduct of the home computer revolution is the growing number of outdated computers. Between 1997 and 2003, there were an estimated 254 million obsolete computers in the U.S. Projections show another 250 million will become obsolete between 2004 and 2007, though the annual number of outdated machines is expected to level off at around 63 million by 2005, according to the National Safety Council.

What is the fate of the used home computer in the U.S.? Most—an estimated 75 percent—are believed to be stockpiled in people's homes, typically in basements, attics, or garages. Fourteen percent are recycled or reused. And, surprisingly, only 11 percent are buried in landfills.

Misperceptions Fuel Fear over E-Waste

Concern over the rapid growth of used computers and what to do with them once they expire has placed the issue of how best to handle electronic waste—or "e-waste"—at the forefront of waste policy at the federal, state, and local levels. Increasingly, propaganda fueled by politically driven environmental activists and a misinformed media is turning concern into hysteria. Fears are largely based on the following myths:

Electronic waste is growing at a rapid and uncontrollable rate and is the fastest growing portion of the municipal waste stream. While the amount of e-waste has been increasing, it remains a tiny percent of the total municipal solid waste stream. According to the Environmental Protection Agency (EPA), e-waste—including discarded TVs, VCRs, DVD players, and audio systems, as well as personal computers, fax machines, and printers—constituted only 1 percent of the total municipal solid waste stream in 1999, the first year EPA calculated electronics discards. Data for 2001 again showed electronic devices had not increased as a percent of total municipal waste but remained at 1 percent.

Nor is e-waste growing at a rapid rate. National Safety Council (NSC) data show that the number of discarded computers will level off by 2005 at 63 million, and will then begin to decline. While improved technology can quickly make machines obsolete, it can also extend the lifespan of the next generation of computers. More powerful microchips will soon provide machines with much greater capacity.

Computers buried in landfills endanger public health because they contain toxic materials such as lead, cadmium, and mercury that can leak out into the soil and groundwater. Cathode ray tubes (CRTs), the most common type of computer display monitor, typically contain four pounds of lead to protect users from the tubes' x-rays, the same way a lead vest protects patients who have x-rays. Because lead is a health risk at high exposure levels, many lawmakers are rushing to ban display monitors and other electronics from municipal landfills, fearing that the lead and other toxic metals can leak out into the ground soil. Overwhelmingly, lawmakers and the popular press point to the work of Timothy Townsend, Associate Professor of Environmental Engineering Sciences at the University of Florida and a leading expert on solid waste, who has been studying for over six years the potential for lead to leak out—or "leach"—from computer monitors, TVs, and other electronic components into the ground soil.

But incredibly, the media has only reported on Townsend's earlier research using the questionable Toxicity Characteristic Leaching Procedure [TCLP] test, a method used by the EPA that attempts to simulate the conditions of a landfill under a worst-case lab test by soaking tiny samples of e-waste in an acid solution and testing their levels of toxicity. Townsend himself concluded in his 1999 report that although his tests showed that 21 of 30 color monitors failed the EPA-defined regulatory limit, the EPA's leaching procedure tests do not mimic what actually occurs in landfills, and "the authors do not attempt to draw conclusions beyond [the specific results of the lab test] in regard to the implications of the lead leaching from CRTs." He also wrote: "The fact that the [EPA's] TCLP test may not represent the true condition of CRTs upon disposal was not an issue of discussion in this research;" and "the leachate concentrations measured [by the EPA lab test method] may not accurately reflect the concentrations observed under typical landfill conditions." Yet newspaper write-ups following the study's release reported only the dangers of lead from electronic monitors in landfills and triggered a panic among many policymakers and lawmakers calling for a ban of all CRTs from landfills.

Ignoring New Tests

Recognizing the EPA test's potential inadequacy in replicating landfill conditions, Townsend and his colleague Yong-Chul

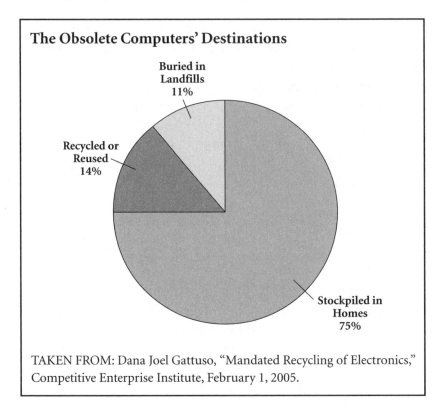

The Obsolete Computers' Destinations

Buried in
Landfills
11%

Recycled or
Reused
14%

Stockpiled in
Homes
75%

TAKEN FROM: Dana Joel Gattuso, "Mandated Recycling of Electronics,"
Competitive Enterprise Institute, February 1, 2005.

Jang conducted a new test in 2003, using 11 actual landfills containing electronic waste and other municipal waste and debris. Specifically, they tested soil from landfills containing waste from color TV and computer monitors, shown in his previous EPA lab tests to leach the highest levels of lead. They also tested soil containing waste from home computer circuit boards, which also contain lead. Comparing the landfills' concentrations of heavy metals in the ground-soil waste—called "leachate"—with levels from the earlier EPA lab test, Townsend found concentrations of lead from the landfilled computer monitor leachate to average only 4.1 milligrams per liter (mg/L)—that's less than 1 percent of what the laboratory studies suggested would be the case (lab tests suggested the monitors would leak 413 mg/L of lead in leachate).

Similarly, he found only 2.2 mg/L of lead in landfill leachate from computer circuit boards—a little more than one percent of the 162 mg estimated in lab tests.

Hence, it is highly likely that actual landfill releases of these heavy metals are far lower than EPA estimates. These differences are far from minimal. As Townsend concludes: "For those state and local governmental agencies wrestling with whether to ban discarded electronics from landfills, the results of this work suggest that lead leaching from [computer circuit boards] and [TV and computer monitors] will be less than might be estimated using EPA's TCLP results." Even more importantly, concentrations from his landfill samples were comfortably below EPA's standards of 5.0 mg/L. Yet it is important to note that these materials would not even enter the environment, since landfill operators collect and dispose of it in a safe manner.

Townsend is further researching leachate and waste settlement from actual landfills. His current study—due to be completed later this year [2005]—involves constructing landfills and filling them with simulated municipal solid waste containing e-waste. But on the overall question of whether e-waste leaches in landfills, Townsend says "there is no compelling evidence."

Other recent studies confirm that lead and other metals contained in landfills are safely contained. A year-long study by the Solid Waste Association of North America (SWANA) Applied Research Foundation, released in March 2004, concludes that heavy toxic metals, including lead, do not pose an existing or future health threat in municipal solid waste landfills. The foundation reviewed existing research and concluded that landfills' natural conditions, such as precipitation and absorption, provide chemical reactions and interactions that prevent heavy metals from dissolving into the soil. They concluded that out of 130,200 tons of heavy metals placed in municipal landfills in 2000 from electronics, batteries, thermometers, and pigments, almost all—98 percent—was lead. Cadmium and mercury made up the remaining amount. According to the authors, "The study presents extensive data that show that heavy metal concentrations in leachate and landfill gas are generally far below the limits that have been established to protect human health and the environment." The report was peer reviewed by an independent panel of researchers in the field, including Timothy Townsend. Oddly, neither this report nor Townsend's recent research comparing EPA lab tests' leachate with actual landfill leachate was ever reported by the general media.

A Lack of Evidence

Even if the natural conditions that prevent leaching did not occur, the sophisticated engineering and monitoring of today's modern municipal landfills, governed by stringent state and federal regulations and performance standards, prevents lead and other heavy metals from leaching. MSW [Municipal Solid Waste] landfills are constructed with thick layers of clay and thick, puncture-resistant liners that keep waste from coming into contact with soil and groundwater. Also, landfills today are constructed with a leachate collection system—a system of pipes that carries any excess leachate out of the landfill and into a separate leachate collection pond where it is then tested and treated. In addition, landfills are surrounded by groundwater monitoring stations which capture samples of groundwater and continuously test for any possible leaks.

In summary, there is no scientific evidence that substances from e-waste present a discernable risk to human health or the environment when disposed of in municipal landfills. Yet widespread fear that lead and other metals in landfills can leach and present a health hazard has provoked lawmakers in a handful of states—California, Maine, Massachusetts, and Minnesota—to ban desktop display monitors from landfills; another half a dozen have pending legislation.

Ironically, the problem is not so much electronic waste itself, but what to do with the enormous quantities of e-waste if lawmakers choose to ban it from landfills. Furthermore, lead and other compounds are considered by some experts to be safer when contained in landfills than during the recycling process when they become exposed. Finally, the cost difference is astronomical. Where a ton of e-waste can cost $500 to recycle, it costs only $40 to landfill.

Sensationalist Rhetoric

Exporting e-waste to developing countries exposes those countries to hazardous waste and toxics, forcing them to choose between "poverty and poison." In 2002, the environmental advocacy groups Basel Action Network and Silicon Valley Toxics Coalition released a scathing study on the methods and conditions of e-waste recovery in developing countries, claiming widespread abuse and mishandling of the toxic components of e-waste. According to the report, *Exporting Harm: The High-Tech Trashing of Asia,* 50 to 80 percent of e-waste collected in the United States for recycling is exported to developing countries. The groups' investigators—who traveled to China, India, and Pakistan—reported that the misuse of e-waste is polluting the environment and "very likely . . . seriously harming human health."

The paper's sensationalistic rhetoric—for example, "free trade in hazardous waste leaves the poorer peoples of the world with an untenable choice between poverty and poison;" and "the export of e-waste remains a dirty little secret of the high tech revolution"—ignited a nationwide campaign to ban further exports and to force manufacturers to take back and recycle their products. Yet no one questioned the report's findings, particularly whether the extreme conditions it described were prevalent throughout Asia.

Ironically, the thousands of tons of computers and other electronics shipped out of the United States to developing countries is the direct result of the rush to ban desktops and other electronics from landfills in this country. The U.S. computer recycling market simply isn't big enough to handle the large amount of e-waste increasingly banned from municipal landfills. That's not the case in developing countries where markets for electronic components and recyclables thrive due to the large demand for labor. Whereas the cost to recycle a home computer in the U.S. is $20, it only costs $4 in developing countries such as India. And for the workers in these poor countries, it can mean the difference between making a living or remaining unemployed.

The widely exaggerated and, in some cases, bogus assumptions concerning the dangers of used computers are creating widespread panic among policy makers who view the issue of e-waste as a desperate and uncontrollable situation. Moreover, these fears are driving perverse and harmful policy objectives in a frantic attempt to solve a non-existent crisis.

Periodical Bibliography

The following articles have been selected to supplement the diverse views presented in this chapter.

George Black — "Life in the Fast Lane," *OnEarth*, Spring 2007.

Deborah Cameron — "Lust for Upgrades Builds a Mountain of E-Waste," *Sydney Morning Herald*, April 16, 2007.

Charles Fishman — "Message in a Bottle," *Fast Company*, July 2007.

Wendee Holtcamp — "My 30 Days of Consumer Celibacy," *OnEarth*, Summer 2007.

Ted Nordhaus and Michael Shellenberger — "Second Life: A Manifesto for a New Environmentalism," *New Republic*, September 24, 2007.

Rachel Nowak — "'Total Recycling' Aims To Make Landfill History," *New Scientist*, October 20, 2007.

Chad Puterbaugh — "Plastic Grocery Bags: Keep Out of Reach of the Environment," *The BG News* [Bowling Green University], January 26, 2007.

Sascha Segan — "Reduce, Reuse, That's It," *PC Magazine*, October 2, 2007.

Henrik Selin and Stacy D. VanDeveer — "Raising Global Standards: Hazardous Substances and E-Waste Management in the European Union," *Environment*, December 2006.

Clark Semmes — "Time to Ban Stores from Giving Away Plastic Bags," *Baltimore Sun*, June 10, 2008.

Skaidra Smith-Heisters — "Paper Grocery Bags Require More Energy Than Plastic Bags," *Reason*, April 17, 2008.

USA Today — "Our View on the Environment: Plastic-Bag Ban Full of Holes," April 2, 2007.

OPPOSING
VIEWPOINTS®
SERIES

What Policies Will Improve the Environment?

Chapter Preface

The goal of early environmentalists was to preserve wildlife and wilderness. These goals broadened in the 1950s and 1960s as people became more concerned about the impact of air and water pollution and the disposal of waste. In recent years, people, businesses, and organizations once considered environmental opponents are now joining the movement or at least taking environmental concerns more seriously than ever before. According to writer Tom Price, "In the burgeoning, new environmental movement, a growing number of people are perceiving threats to the environment, businesses are jumping on the conservation bandwagon and environmentalists are joining hands with groups they once crossed swords with."

Examples of these new environmental actors abound. For example, FedEx is now using fuel efficient hybrid delivery trucks. The conservative National Association of Evangelicals is urging governments to encourage fuel efficiency, reduce pollution, protect wildlife, and promote the sustainable use of resources, proclaiming a "sacred responsibility to steward the Earth." Staunch environmentalists such as British chemist James Lovelock, famous for the hypothesis that the Earth acts as a self-sustaining organism, now embrace nuclear power as "the only green solution."

What factors led to this monumental shift in the environmental movement? Some analysts assert that many of these new environmental actors have been spurred by concerns that global warming poses a real and potentially catastrophic threat to life on Earth. According to David Yarnold, executive vice president of Environmental Defense, "The sense of urgency has grown. And the more people learn about climate change, the more they want to know what they can do." Indeed, public opinion has shifted. A July 2006 Pew Research Center poll reported that 70 percent of Americans said there is solid evidence of global warming and 74 percent said it constitutes a serious or somewhat serious problem. Moreover, nearly 60 percent of Americans wanted the federal government to make energy and the environment top priorities. Thus, some commentators claim, the other factor that has led to a change in the environmental movement, at least in the United States, is that the federal government has failed to act. According to Michael Brune, executive director of the Rainforest Action Network, "There's been an appalling vacuum of leaderships coming from [Washington]—on both sides of the aisle." Brune asserts that while no one expected former President George W. Bush or most Republicans to be environmental leaders, "even most Democrats haven't been stepping up and showing an appropriate level of response to the environmental threats we face." In the absence of action in Washington, Brune maintains, "You're seeing a lot of others trying to show leadership."

The cry for environmental action continues to swell. According to a 2006 Harris Poll, three-quarters of American's feel that "protecting the environment is so important that requirements and standards cannot be too high, and continuing environmental improvements must be made regardless of cost." While these calls for action grow, analysts such as the authors in the following chapter debate what policies will best improve the environment.

> *"Many of the solutions to our environ-*
> *mental challenges are well within*
> *reach, if we work together."*

Environmental Activism Unites People for the Good of the Environment

Carl Pope

Activists are putting aside their differences to protect the envi-
ronment, claims Carl Pope in the following viewpoint. Indeed,
he maintains, the environmental movement has some new faces.
For example, Pope explains, ranchers are working with conserva-
tion groups to fight increased gas and oil drilling in the West,
and hunters and anglers are the most vocal advocates of wet-
lands protection. Everyone has an interest in protecting the envi-
ronment, he asserts, and environmental values are universal val-
ues that unite rather than divide. Pope is executive director of
the Sierra Club, one of the first environmental organizations.

As you read, consider the following questions:

1. What has been the result of Bernadine Edwards' concern about pollution, in Pope's opinion?

Carl Pope, "A New Environmentalism: Could a New Green Ethic Provide Common Cause in Our Deeply Divided Nation?" *American Prospect*, October 2005, pp. A22–23. Copyright © 2005 The American Prospect, Inc. All rights reserved. Reproduced with permission from *American Prospect*, 11 Beacon Street, Suite 1120, Boston, MA 02108.

2. How does the National Council of Churches describe stewardship of the Earth?

3. In the author's view, why have labor unions taken up the cause of protecting the environment?

Mclean County, Kentucky, is so red that political operatives might call it crimson. You can't get much further from the image of a latte-drinking liberal than Bernadine Edwards, a local school-bus driver. She speaks with a soft Kentucky lilt as she looks out over the green valley that has been in her family for more than 60 years. "Something here just ain't right," she says.

Voicing Outrage

What's wrong is the pollution that has slowly ruined her family's life, forcing her to wear a respiratory mask when she gardens outside and making her give up her seat on the porch swing next to her house. In just a few short years, Tyson Foods has built 98 factories within a three-mile radius of Bernadine's home, pumping so much toxic ammonia into the air that Bernadine has sealed her windows and shut her family inside. And when the [George W.] Bush administration began meeting behind closed doors with the poultry industry to craft a deal that would let it off the hook for cleaning up the pollution it causes, Bernadine and other rural residents joined up to voice their outrage. Leaving Kentucky, she traveled to the East Coast for the first time so she could lobby administration officials in Washington about the need to put public-health considerations ahead of polluter profits.

Bernadine's concern about pollution and its consequences for the health of her family has trumped party politics and could provide a common cause in our deeply divided country. It looks like the bridge between red America and blue America just might be green.

The truth is, this country is not as split as many would have us believe. Our values unite us more than they divide us.

We all care about our families, our kids, and our communities, no matter where we are on the political spectrum. We like knowing that there are solutions to our problems and that progress is possible. We believe that two heads are better than one, especially when the two heads see things a little differently. We value free speech and public participation and the well-being of all Americans, not just people who live in certain states. And, like Bernadine Edwards, people on all sides of the spectrum will speak out when they see injustice—especially when that injustice is something felt as viscerally as the air our children breathe and the water we drink.

Beltway strategists [in Washington, D.C.,] might not want us to see it, but if you look around this country you will see more and more examples of how unusual allies are putting aside their political differences and coming together. Americans who can't agree on gun control or abortion are finding common cause in the need to protect our air, water, and land.

Take, for example, the ecumenical Christian network that recently sent a letter to President [George W.] Bush with the line, "Protection of the global climate is an essential requirement for faithful human stewardship of God's creation on Earth." The National Council of Churches, which represents more than 100,000 congregations nationwide, has begun to describe stewardship of the earth as a critical "moral value." And the growing Interfaith Power & Light program has helped more than 300 congregations in California alone conserve energy and has prevented 40 million pounds of carbon dioxide from entering the atmosphere nationwide.

It's not just religious groups, either. Hunters and anglers are the most vocal proponents of wetlands protection, and they represent a formidable obstacle to anyone proposing to weaken protections. In South Dakota, Indian Creek is a beautiful open area of steep canyons and gullies, and a popular destination for big-game hunting of deer and antelope. The Sierra Club is working with Safari Club International and

Focusing on Communities

Popular support can deepen if the concerns for global warming are persuasively tied to the everyday concerns of citizens and to their hopes for a better future. By focusing on community investment as a means of promoting clean energy, support for such concerns connects not just with a generalized sympathy for the environment but also resonates with a far more salient concern for the future of families and communities.

John M. Meyer, "The Afterlife of Environmentalism,"
The American Prospect, *October 2005.*

Backcountry Hunters and Anglers to designate the area as the first-ever grassland wilderness area. And no one is more excited about this than Indian Creek's odd couple, Jeff Olson and Carl Stonecipher—two local hunters on the board of the Blackhills Sportsmen's Club—one a passionate Democrat, the other a staunch Republican. Despite their political differences, both are firmly committed to the idea of protecting wilderness for future generations.

Joining Forces with Foes

Historic foes are joining forces in communities across our country, even in the Wild West. Western ranchers and my organization [the Sierra Club] have set aside our differences to fight a common threat, the surge in gas and oil drilling on federal and Indian land. In New Mexico's San Juan Basin, the number of wells in the region has jumped 15 percent in five years. Cattleman Chris Velasquez, whose family has ranched in the area for more than a century, says sloppy drilling practices—such as leaving pools of toxic antifreeze—endanger the cattle. And conservationists say installing roads and drilling pads damages the piñon- and juniper-covered hills. Elsewhere in the region, ranchers and environmentalists are partnering to protect the land—opposing drilling in Wyoming's Powder River Basin and Montana's Rocky Mountain Front, for example.

These strong alliances are developing in cities as well as rural communities. Labor unions have taken up the environment as a cause; they know better than anyone that developing clean-energy technologies will create quality jobs. And Latino and African American families continue to be the ones on the front lines battling air and other pollution that disproportionately affects their communities.

Residents of a predominantly African American neighborhood in the nation's capital have taken action to reconnect their community to the Anacostia River. Considered one of America's most endangered waterways, the Anacostia is Washington, D.C.'s "forgotten river." Older community members remember swimming and fishing in it, but heavy-metal contamination and sewage overflow have left local fish deformed and dangerous to eat. The Anacostia, however, remains a focal point for the neighborhoods nearby. African American citizen groups in the heart of the inner city are coming together to fight for improved water quality and increased access to the riverfront.

Not Your Typical Conservationists

The environmental movement is full of other new faces—and they differ from the image that you may have in your head of a "typical conservationist." Consider the recent work the Sierra club has done to protect mothers and children from mercury poisoning. Mercury is a dangerous toxin that causes developmental problems and learning disabilities. A byproduct of coal-fired power plants, it rains down into our rivers and makes its way into our bodies via contaminated fish. One in six American women already has enough mercury in her body to put a baby at risk. Across the country, my organization has been hosting community testing events, often at beauty salons, where mothers can get a strand of hair tested and find out how much mercury is in their bodies and what they can do about it. The response has been overwhelming—and not just in big, "liberal" cities. In Salt Lake City, the line of 150 moms snaked so far out the door that the salon couldn't accommodate everyone. In Bismarck, North Dakota, dozens of women showed up at a local park to get tested. And in Virginia, women brought their kids with them to the salon and asked how they could make a difference. "This is not just about tuna," a mother named Julia Smith said. "We have to make the government accountable for cleaning up the power plants."

The bottom line is that these days, the most compelling voices for environmental stewardship are as likely to be those of a mother, a minister, a nurse, or a union shop worker. And what binds them together are American values stronger than hatred or anger or fear. We don't have to buy into the idea that this is an all-or-nothing game, half of our country wins, half loses. We need to tell fewer stories about victims and more about heroes, about the men and women who are affecting real, lasting change.

A Unified Hope for Change

Clearly, we face challenges. There are undeniable obstacles in the way of this vision being carried out—namely, a defiantly pro-business, anti-regulatory administration in Washington. But across the spectrum, a growing chorus is calling for a halt to policies and practices that put polluters before the public.

In recent days, our nation has been shocked and saddened by images of families struggling to survive in the aftermath of Hurricane Katrina. This disaster will test the limits of our national resources, and national unity and grass-roots partnerships like the ones described here will be more imperative than ever in our history. In addition to being a human and economic tragedy, Katrina is an environmental disaster of unprecedented proportions. Although the extent of the environmental devastation remains unknown, it is clear the storm is a wake-up call and a warning not to repeat the mistakes of the past. America, Louisiana, and the Gulf Coast have an opportunity to be visionary and think well into the future in our recovery efforts. In rebuilding New Orleans and the Gulf Coast, we can work with unions to help make America more energy independent—by using "green building" practices that rely on conservation and renewable sources of energy, for example. We can work with churches and associations to ensure that every citizen, rich or poor, can live in safe, healthy neighborhoods. And we can rethink how toxic chemicals are stored and shipped through our communities.

We have learned over and over again that everyone has a stake when it comes to protecting our air, water, and natural places. The values we are talking about—like fairness, responsibility, health, and safety—are universal. And many of the solutions to our environmental challenges are well within reach, if we work together. Thirty-five years after the first Earth Day [in 1970], the movement for cleaner and safer communities is more alive than ever. The vibrant partnerships that are flourishing in grass-roots campaigns across the country are proof that we all have a stake in a healthier future and a legacy for our children.

"When we try to pick out anything by itself," John Muir famously said, "we find it hitched to everything else in the universe." That's truer today than ever.

> *"Man's ingenuity, which is at the heart of individual freedom of expression and development of ideas, is what the environmentalists seek to restrict."*

Environmental Activism Restricts Individual Freedom

Thomas A. Moser

Environmental activists create public hysteria that leads to government controls that in turn restrict human ingenuity, argues Thomas A. Moser in the following viewpoint. Policymakers should make decisions on how best to protect the environment based on reason, not fear, he claims. Lawmakers should weigh the relative dangers of environmental concerns carefully before enacting overreaching laws, Moser maintains. He reasons that free societies educate people about the relative dangers rather than make choices for them. Moser is a consulting professional engineer.

As you read, consider the following questions:

1. In Moser's view, what is true as long as man is free to use the resources and the intelligence he has been given?

Thomas A. Moser, "Protecting the Environment," *Modern Age*, Winter 2005, pp. 89–91. Copyright © 2005 Intercollegiate Studies Institute Inc. Reproduced by permission.

2. According to the author, what is the gospel of the environmentalist?

3. How does the perceived horror of asbestos waste money, in the author's opinion?

I would like to comment on the subject raised by Professor John R.E. Bliese in [the Winter 2000] issue of *Modern Age*. The theme of the article, "Taking the Lead in Environmentalism," is that conservatives should "come to terms with environmentalism and environmental issues." Setting the stage with quotations from highly respected conservative writers, he proceeds to chastise conservative writers for not dealing with this subject, censuring them by using phrases like "virulent anti-environmental attitude" and "'conservative' politicians and pundits and entertainers" (emphasis added). From this he posits that the libertarians are ideologues whose "ideas tend to get lost in their utopian rhetoric and blind worship of markets."

Restricting Ingenuity

Bliese's real concern becomes clear as the focus of the article becomes more cosmic with assumptions and predictions regarding irreversible alterations of the ecosystem. Listing changes in the atmosphere, he accepts without question some of the most radical predictions and calculations of contemporary environmentalists and ecologists. In accepting the proposition that man, in the normal course of using and developing processes for his use of natural resources, is capable of making changes that the Creator of the Universe has not anticipated is presumptuous indeed. There may be a possibility that the end of the world will come about by some nuclear holocaust, but short of this, change is inevitable and will be continuous as long as man is free to use the resources and the intelligence he has been given. This type of use of man's ingenuity, which is at the heart of individual freedom of expression and develop-

ment of ideas, is what the environmentalists seek to restrict and/or replace with a system of governmental controls. European statist governments use this type of restriction on individual activity with the consequent repression of individual entrepreneurial activity, and reduction of individual expression, that characterizes restrictive societies.

There is a tension in this world which manifests itself in many ways and on many levels. This is the tension between good and evil, between the representative forces of good and evil in any situation or debate. At the governmental level it is between a Government of Principles and a Government of Earthly Power. Think of the representative Government of Principles as the Founding Government of these United States and contrast it with the Government of Earthly Power as the Communist Government of Josef Stalin. One proclaims the worth of the individual with inherent powers granted by his Creator, the other proclaims the supreme worth of the government as the answer to all of mankind's problems and that the individual has no worth other than to serve the superior aims of the state. The earthly power government does not tolerate men of principle nor the religions which proclaim these principles.

On the level of science we see this tension in the respect for the earth as a creation of a superior being on the one hand, and, on the other, to the respect for the planning of human science that is proclaimed as the only possible hope for continued survival of the planet. Thus, in analyzing Bliese's article we see that for him the only hope for a viable earth is trust in science and computer models which predict the future. This is the gospel of the environmentalist which proclaims that all actions and activities must be subject to the approval of the scientists.

An Environmentalist's Approach

Certainly there is a need for a conservative approach to environmentalism. The key word here is conservative. There is no need to make radical changes in the operative science and industry of our country as the environmentalists proclaim. There is a pressing need to adopt a serious and sensible approach to improving the environment by carefully analyzing problems and accepting sensible and scientifically sound solutions. In order for this to happen our society must have a standard for determining and accepting scientific truths. Currently scientific truth seems to be the province of a legal community in pursuit of monetary gain, rather than a respect for proven scientific fact. The environmental activist approach is to create fear and hysteria by proclaiming an inevitable apocalypse if we continue to use materials, products, and processes that have been serving mankind for decades and in some cases even centuries.

Examples abound, cigarettes and tobacco products are now anathema [a curse] though they have been in common use for decades. Yes, there are definite harms in the use of these products, but a free society will rely on education not proscription. Asbestos is a valuable product that was used for many years. It can still serve a valuable purpose if properly applied and handled, but the environmentalists and their mercenary allies have made it a scare word. We can no longer use it sensibly, and essentially not at all, due to manufactured hysteria and the resultant liability problems. Mercury, a toy generations ago, is now treated as an aggressive horror waiting to pounce on an unsuspecting populace. Lead is actively pursuing our children to rob them of their ability to think and retain information. For the environmental activist the relative danger of these things is not to be considered or evaluated. They must be eliminated from society and banned from the market place.

More currently, mold has become a scare word, or more specifically to use current jargon, "toxic mold." Allowing petroleum products in even minute amounts to return to the soil from which they originated is anathema. The required clean up, removal, and treatment of "contaminated soil," whether it is in a sensitive location next to a water source or in a remote wasteland, seems irrelevant, and is costing society millions of dollars. The same is true of the draconian insistence on the removal of asbestos or asbestos-containing materials from the nation's school buildings, regardless of the quantity, type, or percentage involved. Money that is needed for education is being wasted on these removals, not because of a proven danger, but simply because of a perceived horror of "asbestos" and the legal liability that this perception represents.

Environmental activists and the sensation-hungry media are robbing us of the use of materials and products through a public relations scare campaign. Evaluation of risk is no longer an acceptable procedure. Yes, there is an urgent need for conservatives to address environmental issues. Conservative voices are needed to bring logic and good sense into the picture. Mandated removal procedures that logically should cost thousands are costing millions due to the establishment of excessively stringent and unnecessary standards, perceptions of legal liability, rules, and laws. Politicians are unable to make sensible laws due to the hysteria that has been created by sensationalist news stories, histrionic lawyers, and confused juries.

A Practical Approach

The practical aspects of determining which processes and materials are dangerous and evaluating risks associated with their use is a job for scientists and engineers operating under a governmental and judicial system that provides an atmosphere of reason and a method of logically evaluating and approving the resulting decisions. Deciding these questions in courtrooms under highly emotional circumstances can never produce intelligent and reliable results.

The challenge, then, for the conservative thinker and politician is to promote the principles and political atmosphere that can bring logic and common sense back into the government, its legal system, and the media. The relative danger of exposure to various materials can be determined, codified, and promulgated. The toxicity of dangerous or hazardous materials is available in the technical literature as are the carcinogenic properties. Such data are ignored or are too complicated for evaluation in the nation's courtrooms. The present atmosphere is not hospitable to the idea of accepted scientific data no matter how reliable or completely researched and investigated. Conservatives must help the country discard relativism and return to an acceptance of immutable facts in contrast to the currently popular concept that there is no certain truth, no hard and fast right and wrong.

> "*Better product choices . . . enable us to maintain the way of life to which we're accustomed without overtaxing the planet's ability to sustain it.*"

Buying Green Products Will Improve the Environment

Jenny Shank interview with Josh Dorfman

In the following viewpoint, writer Jenny Shank interviews Josh Dorfman, author of The Lazy Environmentalist *and host of a radio show of the same name. Dorfman asserts that because people are going to continue to consume, one way to improve the environment is to buy more environmentally conscious—green— products. Indeed, businesses that want to promote environmental change should appeal both to people's environmental awareness and to their self-interest, Dorfman claims. Developing eco-friendly choices will help push America's economy in a green direction, he concludes.*

As you read, consider the following questions:

1. According to Dorfman, what is a poor way to market going green?

2. Using what words in the same sentence would have been the butt of a joke in 2003, in Dorfman's view?

3. What does Dorfman claim will never happen among the millions of Americans who drive SUVs?

The title of Josh Dorfman's new guide to environmentally aware products, *The Lazy Environmentalist*, appealed to me immediately because it seemed to encapsulate my approach to environmentalism. I tried to start a compost pile recently and it didn't go well; I failed to stir it and incorporate enough dirt and every time I visit it I am attacked by seething swarms of fruit flies. Luckily Dorfman has a product recommendation to solve my problem (see below). In 2003, Dorfman founded Vivavi, a company that provides stylish furniture built with the sustainable materials, and soon thereafter launched his guide to finding green-built homes and materials, *Modern Green Living*. He also hosts the daily "Lazy Environmentalist" show on Sirius Satellite Radio. I recently interviewed Josh Dorfman, via email about his lazy ways, some solutions to a few environmental dilemmas, and how environmental "gloom-and-doom is a really lousy marketing campaign."

New West: How did you first become interested in the environmentally conscious products that you write about in The Lazy Environmentalist?

Josh Dorfman: I worked in China in the mid-1990's, where I traveled around the country selling bicycle locks for a company called Kryptonite. I saw a country transforming from a billion bicyclists toward a billion car drivers. I'm not sure that the planet's ecosystems can handle the pollution from another billion cars on the road. So I started thinking that we all need to be presented with better product choices that enable us to maintain the way of life to which we're accustomed without overtaxing the planet's ability to sustain it.

Lazy Solutions

Do you find yourself thinking about the environmental impact of everything you do, from flushing the toilet to turning on the light in a room?

Yes, but I don't find myself always doing something about it because I'm somewhat lazy. That's why I seek out products that make environmental choices easy. Because if they work for me, I think they'll work for others too.

What is the laziest thing you've ever done in the name of the environment?

I switched over to 100% wind power for my apartment by checking a few boxes and making a few mouse clicks on the website of my power utility. If you go to www.epa.gov/greenpower you'll find 600 power utilities throughout the U.S. that make getting clean, green energy in your home a snap. It only costs me about $6 more per month for my apartment, but now every time I sit on my couch and turn on the TV I get to derive tremendous satisfaction from the fact that the TV is running on wind power.

Not Your Typical Environmentalist

The bio on your website describes you as "not your typical environmental activist." Do you have much interaction with more "typical" environmental activists? What do you think Julia Butterfly Hill, for example (the woman who sits in trees), would think of your approach? Are you all on the same side, or are there environmentalists who take exception to your approach?

I'm not sure what she would think, but I think she's sexy, and I like that she always dresses in black. I believe we're all on the same side though there are people in the environmental community who take exception to my approach. I'm simply suggesting that since we all consume products every single day, we can use that power to effect positive environmental change by making better decisions. And fortunately, the green product choices have gotten so much better that it's really pretty easy to start leading a green lifestyle on a daily basis. There is a portion of the environmental movement, however, that seems more concerned with being "right" than with being effective. I don't think those folks are particularly fond of me.

Environmental Choices

You seem to be upbeat, not as doom-gloom as some environmentalists. Do you think that a more positive attitude toward the problem of living in an environmentally conscious way will better attract people who normally wouldn't think about these things?

Yes because gloom-and-doom is a really lousy marketing campaign. I want people to get excited about going green and they should because what could be cooler than an automatic composter from Naturemill that comes in a compact, sleek, silver case, sits inconspicuously on your kitchen floor, doesn't smell bad, and does the job for you? People get excited about that kind of innovation because it lets them be part of the solution without having to change how they live. In fact, it improves how they live.

It seems like in many cases, the product option that is better for the environment is more expensive. Have you come across any examples where the environmental option is cheaper?

Check out Method cleaning products. They're non-toxic, biodegradable and packaged in the best looking cleaning bottles ever. They're also sold at Target and they're inexpensive. Or look at Terracycle organic plant food that is extremely potent and very cheap. It happens to come from worm poop and be packaged in reused 20 oz. soda bottles. It's available at Home Depot. Walmart is selling 100% organically grown, 300-thread-count cotton sheet sets for less than $40. There are quite a few options available.

Eco Innovation

I've found that it's sometimes difficult to weigh the environmental impact of a choice, especially when it's coupled with financial considerations. For example, in Colorado we have water shortages, so it has been suggested that choosing disposable diapers is better than cloth because of all the water it takes to wash them. You recommend gDiapers, which have a cloth and flushable insert combo, but they are more expensive than disposables (can you tell I have a baby?). How do you take into account all of this stuff? Do you just do the best you can?

We're just at the beginning of a very, exciting phase where more and more eco-friendly choices are going to become available to really push our economy in a green direction and start to solve our environmental challenges. In the interim, I suggest you do what you can. I'd also suggest that gDiapers are really cute and that your baby will be stylin' in them. That's important to a lot of parents.

Do you forsee a time when environmentally conscious products will be made available for people of all income levels? (For now, it seems these products mostly cater to people with higher incomes.)

Yes, and I think it's coming very quickly. When I started Vivavi in 2003 there were very few environmentally conscious products available that had any sense of style. Few people at the time could have conceived that you could use "stylish" and "eco-friendly" in the same sentence without it being the butt of a joke. Four years later we're talking about hundreds and hundreds of stylish, well-conceived, eco-friendly products and services. It's happened unbelievably quickly. The next few years is going to see the pace of eco-friendly product innovation accelerate, and we all will benefit as a result.

Your book includes a chapter on "Death and Dying." Have you discussed planning an eco-burial with your family members? Is this a conversation that you encourage people to have?

No, I haven't and I'm not anticipating the need to do so anytime soon. But when the time is appropriate I will. Choosing an eco-friendly burial requires as much forethought as choosing a conventional burial. No more, no less. That's really the point. We don't have to change how we live or in this case, how we die, just to do right by the planet. That's a good thing because it means that more of us are going to be willing to make these kinds of decisions once we know about them.

The Challenge for Consumers

A critic for the Nashville Scene *said of your book, "...this is a book for people determined to miss the real point: that voracious consumerism is part of what got us into this mess to begin with." How do you respond to that?*

I think it's irrelevant. The reality is that we consume products every day. This is not going to change anytime soon. So we have to find more environmentally conscious ways to consume if we want to maintain our quality of lives and not see them degraded by climate change currently resulting directly from our consumption. However, the solutions have to fit our lifestyles or the great majority of us won't even consider them. For example, millions of people in this country drive SUVs [sport utility vehicles]. Now you could demand that all SUV drivers give up their SUVs and walk to the supermarket. But it's irrelevant because it will never happen. You could demand that they buy compact cars. Some might. Most probably will just call you a Communist and turn up the TV volume. So how do you reach those "voracious consumers?" I think you talk to them about Hybrid SUVs like the Ford Hybrid Explorer that gets 34 miles per gallon and will save them money at the pump. If you want to effect positive change, start appealing to people's enlightened self-interest. We're still very much in the what's-in-it-for-me phase of environmental awareness.

Is there anything you do that is bad for the environment, but you just don't want to give up? For example, I have always relished a good, long shower.

Yes, I take very long showers because it's where I do my best thinking. I installed an Oxygenics low-flow showerhead to mitigate the damage. I also like to crank the A/C [air conditioning] at night to keep my bedroom very cool. I rely upon an Energy Star rated air conditioner that uses less energy. There are product solutions that can help all of us with our environmental shortcomings.

Packaging is what seems to produce the most waste in my household—things that can't be composted or recycled, like plastic takeout boxes, or the plastic that just about everything comes in. Have you come across any solutions to this dilemma?

One of my favorite companies is RecycleBank. Starting with communities in Philadelphia, PA, and Wilmington, Delaware, ReycleBank provides homes with a barcoded garbage container into which all trash recyclables can be thrown. No separation necessary. It's then picked up by a garbage truck that scans and computes the contents of your garbage and awards you RecycleBank dollars for the amount you've recycled. To view how much you've earned, you log on to RecycleBank.com. You can then redeem those dollars at participating retailers like Starbucks, Whole Foods, Timberland, and Patagonia. It's the recycling solution that not only simplifies, but actually pays you to do the right thing.

Does it seem to you that there has been a sea change in the average American's attitude toward the environment lately? Global warming seems to be presented more and more as a scientific reality rather than merely as a theory. Or is this just a change in the media's storyline that hasn't yet entered most people's day-to-day thoughts?

I think that we're starting to reach a consensus in this country that Global Warming is real. But I also think that many people who acknowledge the reality of Global Warming still hope that it will just somehow go away. As a nation, we don't really want to deal with it. We have neither the political leadership nor the political will, which is why I think that for now the environmental solutions presented have to be both effective and painless. So it's precisely these kinds of solutions which I write about in my book.

> *"When wannabe environmentalists try to change purchasing habits without also altering their consumer mind-set, something gets lost in translation."*

Buying Green Products Is an Inadequate Environmental Remedy

Monica Hesse

Buying green is a sign that people recognize the need to protect the environment, claims Monica Hesse in the following viewpoint. However, she argues, consuming green products is not the solution. Consumption will not solve the nation's environmental challenges, Hesse explains. To be truly green means to buy less, not green, she maintains. Replacing products thought to be environmentally unsound increases consumption, which in turn increases environmental problems, she reasons. Hesse is a staff writer for The Washington Post.

As you read, consider the following questions:

1. According to Hesse, into what markets has buying organic seeped?

2. What destiny did economist Victor Lebow lay out for consumers in 1955?

3. What percentage of devout green consumers did not know what the USDA "organic" seal meant, according to a Hartman Group survey?

Congregation of the Church of the Holy Organic, let us buy.

Let us buy Anna Sova Luxury Organics Turkish towels, 900 grams per square meter, $58 apiece. Let us buy the eco-friendly 600-thread-count bed sheets, milled in Switzerland with U.S. cotton, $570 for queen-size.

Let us purge our closets of those sinful synthetics, purify ourselves in the flame of the soy candle at the altar of the immaculate Earth Weave rug, and let us *buy*, buy, buy until we are whipped into a beatific froth of free-range fulfillment.

And let us never consider the other organic option—*not* buying—because the new green *consumer* wants to consume, to be more celadon than emerald, in the right color family but muted, without all the hand-me-down baby clothes and out-of-date carpet.

The Green Consumer Movement

There was a time, and it was pre-Al Gore, when buying organic meant eggs and tomatoes, Whole Foods and farmer's markets. But . . . the word has seeped out of the supermarket and into the home store, into the vacation industry, into the Wal-Mart. Almost three-quarters of the U.S. population buys organic products at least occasionally; between 2005 and 2006 the sale of organic non-food items increased 26 percent, from $744 million to $938 million, according to the Organic Trade Association.

Green is the new black, carbon is the new kryptonite, blah blah blah. The privileged eco-friendly American realized long ago that SUVs [sport utility vehicles] were Death Stars; now we see that our gas-only Lexus is one, too. Best replace it with a 2008 LS 600 *hybrid* for $104,000 (it actually gets fewer miles per gallon than some traditional makes, but, see, it is a hybrid). Accessorize the interior with an organic Sherpa car seat cover for only $119.99.

Consuming until you're squeaky green. It feels so good. It looks so good. It feels so good to look so good, which is why conspicuousness is key.

These countertops are pressed paper.

Have I shown you my recycled platinum engagement ring?. . .

Our inbox has runneth over with giddily organic products: There's the 100 percent Organic Solana Swaddle Wrap, designed to replace baby blankets we did not even know were evil. There's the Valentine's pitch, "Forget Red—The color of love this season is Green!" It is advertising a water filter. There are the all-natural wasabi-covered goji berries, $30 for a snack six-pack, representing "a rare feat for wasabi."

There is the rebirth of *Organic Style* magazine, now only online but still as fashionable as ever, with a shopping section devoted to organic jewelry, organic pet bedding, organic garden decor, which apparently means more than "flowers" and "dirt."

The Culture of Obsolescence

When renowned environmentalist Paul Hawken is asked to comment on the new green consumer, he says, dryly, "The phrase itself is an oxymoron."

Oh ho?

"The good thing is people are waking up to the fact that we have a real [environmental] issue," says Hawken, who co-founded Smith & Hawken but left in 1992, before the $8,000 lawn became de rigueur [standard]. "But many of them are coming to the issue from being consumers. They buy a lot. They drive a lot."

They subscribe, in other words, to a destiny laid out by economist Victor Lebow, writing in 1955: "Our enormously productive economy demands that we make consumption our way of life, that we convert the buying and use of goods into rituals, that we seek our spiritual satisfaction . . . in consumption. . . . We need things consumed, burned up, replaced and discarded at an ever-accelerating rate."

The culture of obsolescence has become so deeply ingrained that it's practically reflexive. Holey sweaters get pitched, not mended. Laptops and cellphones get slimmer and shinier and smaller. We trade up every six months, and to make up for that, we buy and buy and hope we're buying the right *other* things, though sometimes we're not sure: When the Hartman Group, a market research firm, asked a group of devout green consumers what the USDA [U.S. Department of Agriculture] "organic" seal meant when placed on a product, 43 percent did not know. (The seal means that the product is at least 95 percent organic—no pesticides, no synthetic hormones, no sewage sludge, no irradiation, no cloning.)

The Replacement Problem

Which is why, when wannabe environmentalists try to change purchasing habits without also altering their consumer mindset, something gets lost in translation.

Polyester = bad. Solution? Throw out the old wardrobe and replace with natural fibers!

Linoleum = bad. Solution? Rip up the old floor and replace with cork!

Out with the old, in with the green.

It's done with the best of intentions, but all that replacing is problematic. That "bad" vinyl flooring? It was probably less destructive in your kitchens than in a landfill (unless, of course, it was a health hazard). Ditto for the older, but still wearable, clothes.

The Green Illusion

We're in the midst of a green revolution, right? Actually, no. Despite ... the green-branding of products from toothpaste to toilet paper, most consumers are unwilling to pay extra or make sacrifices to be more environmentally friendly. A recent study by the market research firm Yankelovich found that only 13 percent of Americans are passionate about environmental issues—while 29 percent have virtually no interest. For most companies, green products represent only a "niche" opportunity.

Rick Newman, "The Green Mirage,"
U.S. News & World Report, *Oct. 30, 2007.*

And that's not even getting into the carbon footprint left by a nice duvet's 5,000-mile flight from Switzerland. (Oh, all right: a one-way ticket from Zurich to Washington produces about 1,500 pounds of carbon dioxide.)

Really going green, Hawken says, "means having less. It *does* mean less. Everyone is saying, 'You don't have to change your lifestyle.' Well, yes, actually, you *do*."

But, but, but—buying green feels so *guilt less*, akin to the mentality that results in eating 14 of Whole Foods' two-bite cupcakes. Their first ingredient is cane sugar, but in a land of high-fructose panic, that's practically a health food, right? Have another.

"There's a certain thrill, that you get to go out and replace everything," says Leslie Garrett, author of "The Virtuous Consumer," a green shopping guide. "New bamboo T-shirts, new hemp curtains."

Conflicting Feelings

Garrett describes the conflicting feelings she and her husband experienced when trying to decide whether to toss an old living room sofa: "Our dog had chewed on it—there were only so many positions we could put it in" without the teeth marks showing. But it still fulfilled its basic role as a sofa: "We could still sit on it without falling through."

They could still make do. They could still, in this recession-wary economy, where everyone tries to cut back, subscribe to the crazy notion that conservation was about . . . conserving. Says Garrett, "The greenest products are the ones you don't buy."

There are exceptions. "Certain environmental issues trump other issues," Garrett says. "Preserving fossil fuels is more critical than landfill issues." If your furnace or fridge is functioning but inefficient, you can replace it guilt-free.

Ultimately, Garrett and her husband did buy a new sofa (from Ikea—Garrett appreciated the company's ban on carcinogens). But they made the purchase only after finding another home for their old couch—a college student on Craigslist was happy to take it off their hands.

The sofa example is what Josh Dorfman, host of the Seattle radio show "The Lazy Environmentalist," considers to be a best-case scenario for the modern consumer. "Buying stuff is intrinsically wrapped up in our identities," Dorfman says. "You can't change that behavior. It's better to say, 'You're a crazy shopaholic. You're not going to stop being a crazy shopaholic. But if you're going to buy 50 pairs of jeans, buy them from this better place.'"

Then again, his show is called "The Lazy Environmentalist."

Walking Through the Gate

Chip Giller, editor of enviro-blog Grist.org, has a less fatalistic view. He loves that Wal-Mart has developed an organic line.

He applauds the efforts of the green consumer. "Two years ago, who would have thought we'd be in a place where terms like locavore and carbon footprint were household terms?" he says, viewing green consumption as a "gateway" to get more people involved in environmental issues. The important thing is for people to keep walking through the gate, toward the land of reduced air travel, energy-efficient homes and much less stuff: "We're not going to buy our way out of this."

Congregation of the Church of the Holy Organic, let us scrub our sins away with Seventh Generation cleaning products. Let us go ahead and bite into the locally grown apple, and let us replace our incandescent light bulbs with those dreadfully expensive fluorescents.

But yea, though we walk through the valley of the luxury organic, let us purchase no imported Sherpa car seat covers. Let us use the old one, even though it is ugly, because our toddler will spill Pom juice on the organic one just as quickly as on the hand-me-down. Amen.

> *"A potential paradigm shift . . . necessitated by the earth's climate crisis, can point the way out of 'gray capitalism' and into a green, more equitable economy."*

Green Economic Policies Will Improve the Environment and Promote Equality

Preeti Mangala Shekar and Tram Nguyen

Economic policies that train people for green jobs will improve the environment and help the people most threatened by environmental degradation, assert Preeti Mangala Shekar and Tram Nguyen in the following viewpoint. Traditional economic policies that use resources unsustainably hit the poor the hardest, the authors maintain. For example, they argue, toxins are often dumped in poor communities where people have little power to prevent it. However, the authors reason that all people benefit from green economies in which production, human needs, and the environment are more harmonious. Shekar is a feminist journalist, and Nguyen is executive editor of ColorLines.

Preeti Mangala Shekar and Tram Nguyen, "Who Gains from the Green Economy?" *ColorLines*, March/April 2008, p. 18. Copyright © 2008 ColorLines Magazine. Reproduced by permission.

As you read, consider the following questions:

1. According to Shekar and Nguyen, what might happen to some communities if an equitable development model is not defined?

2. In addition to being practitioners, what must communities also do in the green economy, in the authors' view?

3. In *Designing the Green Economy*, how does Brian Milani define green economics?

The Oakland-based Ella Baker Center for Human Rights, with a miniscule staff and budget, worked relentlessly [in 2007] to pass the Green Jobs Act in Congress—a bill that if authorized will direct $125 million to green the nation's workforce and train 35,000 people each year for "green-collar jobs."[1] That summer, Ella Baker Center and the Oakland Alliance also secured $250,000 from the city to build the Oakland Green Jobs Corp, a training program that promises to explicitly serve what is probably the most underutilized resource of Oakland: young working-class men and women of color.

A Paradigm Shift

In these efforts lay a hopeful vision—that the crises-ridden worlds of economics and environmentalism would converge to address the other huge crisis—racism in the United States. It is what some of its advocates call a potential paradigm shift that, necessitated by the earth's climate crisis, can point the way out of "gray capitalism" and into a green, more equitable economy. The engine of this model is driven by the young and proactive leadership of people of color who intend to build a different solution for communities of color.

Van Jones, president of the newly formed Green for All campaign, talks about how earlier waves of economic flourishes didn't much impact Black communities. "When the dot-

1. As of August 2008, the bill has been calendared for but not yet debated in the House.

com boom went bust, you didn't see no Black man lose his shirt," he points out, only half joking. "Black people were the least invested in it."

Climate change is the 21st century's wake-up call to not just rethink but radically redo our economies. Ninety percent of scientists agree that we are headed toward a climate crisis, and that, indeed, it has already started. With the urgent need to reduce carbon emissions, the clean energy economy is poised to grow enormously. This sector includes anything that meets our energy needs without contributing to carbon emissions or that reduces carbon emissions; it encompasses building retrofitting, horticulture infrastructure (tree pruning and urban gardening), food security, biofuels and other renewable energy sources, and more.

It's becoming clear that investing in clean energy has the potential to create good jobs, many of them located in urban areas as state and city governments are increasingly adopting public policies designed to improve urban environmental quality in areas such as solar energy, waste reduction, materials reuse, public transit infrastructures, green building, energy and water efficiency, and alternative fuels.

According to recent research by Raquel Pinderhughes, a professor of Urban Studies at San Francisco State University, green jobs have an enormous potential to reverse the decades-long trend of unemployment rates that are higher for people of color than whites. In Berkeley, California, for example, unemployment of people of color is between 1.5 and 3.5 times that of white people, and the per capita income of people of color is once again between 40 to 70 percent of that of white people.

Pinderhughes defines green-collar jobs as manual labor jobs in businesses whose goods and services directly improve environmental quality. These jobs are typically located in large and small for-profit businesses, nonprofit organizations, social enterprises, and public and private institutions. Most impor-

Creating Green Environmental Communities

As the country faces a growing threat of climate change, environmental- and social-justice activists are uniting to articulate a set of solutions that both overhaul the old, dirty economy and overcome the country's class and race divides. "Greencollar jobs" programs ... have been gaining traction at both the local and federal level, highlighting the need to ensure that [activists who live in poor, violent, and toxic communities] have a role in moving their cities toward a cleaner economy. If the new movement is successful, the green economy could be one that lifts all boats—and breaks down the barriers that have segregated both the environmental community and the country.

Kate Sheppard, "The Green Gap,"
The American Prospect, *May 2008.*

tantly, these jobs offer training, an entry level that usually re-quires only a high school diploma, and decent wages and ben-efits, as well as a potential career path in a growing industry.

Preventing Gentrification

Yet, though green economics present a great opportunity to lift millions of unemployed, underemployed or displaced workers—many of them people of color—out of poverty, the challenge lies in defining an equitable and workable develop-ment model that would actually secure good jobs for margin-alized communities.

"Green economics needs to be eventually policy-driven. If not, the greening of towns and cities will definitely set in mo-tion the wheels of gentrification," Pinderhughes adds. "Without a set of policies that explicitly ensures checks and measures to prevent gentrification, green economics cannot be a panacea for the ills of the current economy that actively displaces and marginalizes people of color, while requiring their cheap labor and participation as exploited consumers."

Sustainable South Bronx is among the leading local organizations designing innovative green economic development projects. These precedents should form the core of state and federal green development and jobs programs. In 2001, Majora Carter, who grew up in the area, one of the most polluted in the country, founded the organization with a focus on building a Greenway along the banks of the South Bronx riverfront. . . .

In 2003, Sustainable South Bronx started Project BEST (Bronx Environmental Stewardship Training) to train local residents, largely young adults, in green collar jobs. The program has become one of the nation's most successful, boasting a 90 percent job placement rate. Project BEST includes 10 weeks of training in a wide range of green activities, including riverbank and wetlands restoration, urban horticulture, green roof installation and maintenance and hazardous waste clean up. Graduates leave the program with six official certifications as well as what Sustainable South Bronx calls a "powerful environmental justice perspective." "We wanted to make sure that people had both the personal and financial stake in the betterment of the environment," said Carter. "They already knew the public health impacts, being a repository for the dirty economy. What they didn't know was that they could also be direct beneficiaries." The program helps people find work afterward, and tracks graduates for at least three years to measure their progress.

Creating a Political Movement

Thus, Sustainable South Bronx builds a constituency for the green economy by creating chances for people to live in it.

These communities have to be prepared not just to become practitioners in the new economy, but also as political actors who propose and fight for legislative solutions. . . .

A movement toward economic justice requires the mobilizing and organizing of the poorest people for greater economic and political power. A good green economic model would surely be one where poor people's labor has considerable economic leverage. "Wal-Mart putting solar panels on its store roofs is not a solution," says Clarke. "We need real solutions and strong measures—carbon taxes on imports from China would considerably reduce the incentive of cheap imports and make a push to produce locally."

"Green economics can create a momentum—a political moment akin to the civil rights movement. But unless workers are organized, any success is likely to be marginal. So the key problem is in organizing a political base," adds Clarke.

Green economics, then, is not just a green version of current economic models but a fundamental transformation, outlines Brian Milani, a Canadian academic and environmental expert who has written extensively on green economics. He writes in his book *Designing the Green Economy*: "Green economics is the economics of the real world—the world of work, human needs, the earth's materials, and how they mesh together most harmoniously. It is primarily about 'use value,' not 'exchange value' or money. It is about quality, not quantity, for the sake of it. It is about regeneration—of individuals, communities, and ecosystems—not about accumulation, of either money or material." . . .

As we have learned in many progressive struggles, communities need to be mobilized and actively involved in generating inclusive policies and pushing policymakers to ensure that green economic development will be just and equitable. Bracken Hendricks, a senior fellow at the Center for American Progress and co-author of *Apollo's Fire: Igniting America's Clean Energy Economy*, says the green economy movement is still in its early stages of building public support. "There is not yet an organized constituency representing the human face of what it means to face climate change. There is an urgent need for a human face, an equity constituency, to enter into the national debate on climate change."

Omar Freilla, founder of Green Worker Cooperative, an organization that actively promotes worker-owned and eco-friendly manufacturing jobs to the South Bronx, is convinced that democracy begins at the workplace where many of us as workers and employees spend most of our time. "The environmental justice movement has been about people taking control of their own communities," he says. "Those most impacted by a problem are also the ones leading the hunt for a solution."

Refining Green Economics

Environmental racism is rooted in a dirty energy economy, a reckless linear model that terminates with the dumping of toxins and wastes in poor communities of color that have the least access to political power to change this linear path to destruction.

Defining and then refining green economics as a way to steer it toward bigger change is at the root of understanding the socio-political and economic possibilities of this moment. Van Jones calls for a historic approach, one that considers the world economy in stages of refinement. "Green capitalism is not the final stage of human development, any more than gray capitalism was. There will be other models and other advances—but only if we survive as a species. But we have to recognize that we are at a particular stage of history, where the choices are not capitalism versus socialism, but green/eco-capitalism versus gray/suicide capitalism. The first industrial revolution hurt both people and the planet, very badly. Today, we do have a chance to create a second 'green' industrial revolution, one that will produce much better ecological outcomes. Our task is to ensure that this green revolution suc-ceeds—and to ensure that the new model also generates much better social outcomes. I don't know what will replace eco-capitalism. But I do know that no one will be here to find out, if we don't first replace gray capitalism."

The people most affected by the injustices of the polluting economy are already helping to lead the way, and it's business at its most unusual.

> "America's Climate Security Act promises all economic pain for little or no environmental gain."

Environmental Laws Threaten American Workers

Ben Lieberman

In the following viewpoint, Ben Lieberman claims that environmental statutes have put many Americans in the unemployment line. Indeed, he argues, global-warming bills such as the proposed Climate Security Act also threaten the livelihood of the American worker. According to one study, the Climate Security Act will sacrifice 500,000 manufacturing jobs. Claims that green-collar jobs will make up for these losses are mistaken, he argues. Lieberman is an energy and environment policy analyst at the Heritage Foundation, a conservative think tank.

As you read, consider the following questions:

1. In Lieberman's opinion, in addition to destroying some jobs outright, what has been the impact of environmental statutes on other jobs?

2. What will happen to most of the workers displaced by the Climate Security Act, in the author's view?

3. In addition to struggling with layoffs and lower-paying jobs, what does the author claim many households will have to endure?

It may be time to put American workers on the endangered-species list. For nearly 40 years, the environmental movement has all but declared war on high-wage, blue-collar jobs, with considerable success. Now, a proposed global-warming bill called the America's Climate Security Act would finish off many of the remaining ones. Green activists and regulators have sent many such working men and women to the unemployment line, or to lower-wage service-sector jobs.

Targeting U.S. Jobs

Shutting down mines kills mining jobs, opposing logging decreases logging jobs, and, naturally, closing factories reduces factory jobs.

Since 1969, more than a dozen environmental statutes, each spawning volumes of unnecessarily costly regulations and litigation, have targeted all manner of industrial activity. Some of these jobs have been destroyed outright, while others have been outsourced to nations with less expensive restrictions or none at all.

But the Climate Security Act, currently debated in the Senate, may do more economic harm than all these past laws put together.

Beginning in 2012, the bill cracks down on emissions of carbon dioxide from burning fossil fuels, which is blamed for global warming. This would raise energy prices significantly. Particularly hard-hit would be energy-intensive industries that rely on coal-fired electricity, such as steel, cement and paper. Also losing out are segments of the chemical industry that depend on natural gas as an energy source and chemical feed-stock. Domestic oil production and refining would be hurt as well.

According to a Heritage Foundation study, the bill would cost a half-million manufacturing jobs by 2018, 1 million by 2022, and more than 2 million by 2027. Of course, most of these displaced workers will eventually find something else to do, but often at lower wages.

Some proponents claim new "green collar" jobs would make up the difference. For example, there will be more work at solar-panel manufacturers and other industries helped by the bill.

A Job-Killing Bill

But these jobs will be swamped by the number of those lost. The Heritage figures are net of any manufacturing jobs gained, and also exclude blue-collar jobs likely to be lost for reasons unrelated to the global-warming bill. The bottom line: This bill is a major job killer.

The impact will disproportionately hurt the working class—both those who have blue-collar jobs already and those who will seek them in the future. For many people, these are the best jobs, and they offer the highest standards of living available. But if this bill passes, their numbers would dwindle considerably.[1]

To add insult to injury, as many households struggle with layoffs and shifts to lower-paying jobs, they also will have to endure higher prices for electricity, natural gas and gasoline thanks to this bill—a costly double whammy. The cost of gasoline alone is expected to rise 29 percent by 2030.

Is there an upside that makes this sacrifice worthwhile? Even if one assumes the worst, environmentally speaking, of global warming, this bill is expected to reduce the Earth's fu-

1. As of August 2008, the Climate Security Act has been put on the calendar but not yet debated in the House.

The Jobs Problem

How do we get ourselves unstuck? Any strategic effort to get at and ultimately reverse these trends must begin by confronting the implications of an obvious truth: whatever people's true feelings about the environment, they will understandably choose jobs over the environment when the two appear to conflict. Air and water pollution, for example, is commonly difficult to deal with at the local level because citizens and political leaders fear the loss of jobs that a challenge to corporate polluters might produce, even when the threat is severe. The citizens of Pigeon River, Tennessee, for instance, chose a few years ago to tolerate potentially carcinogenic emissions by North Carolina's Champion International paper mill because of fear they might otherwise lose 1,000 jobs. A 51-year-old worker who supported keeping the plant open despite the danger spoke for many: "What do you do when you're my age and faced with the prospect of being thrown out on the street?"

If we are unable to solve the jobs problem, there will be continued political opposition to important environmental measures that might cause economic dislocation. On the other hand, to the degree communities can be assured of economic stability, their ability to deal with environmental problems can clearly be greatly enhanced.

Gar Alperovitz,
"You Say You Want a Revolution?"
World Watch, *November/December 2005.*

ture temperature by a small fraction of 1 degree—too small to even verify. And even less so if manufacturing jobs killed here are shipped to developing nations such as China, which is less energy efficient and has far more emissions.

Overall, the America's Climate Security Act promises all economic pain for little or no environmental gain.

The federal government recently listed the polar bear under the Endangered Species Act, claiming that global warming is causing it harm. In reality, the number of polar bears has more than doubled in recent decades. Too bad there are no protections for something that is truly at risk of disappearing—the American blue-collar worker.

Periodical Bibliography

The following articles have been selected to supplement the diverse views presented in this chapter.

Colin Campbell	"The Colour of Money: Corporate Canada Has Awakened to the Huge Benefits in Going Green," *MacLean's*, May 14, 2007.
Paul Davidson	"Getting Gold Out of Green," *USA Today*, April 19, 2007.
Mark Dolliver	"Deflating a Myth: Consumers Aren't As Devoted to the Planet As You Wish They Were," *Brandweek*, May 12, 2008.
Economist	"Waking Up and Catching Up," January 27, 2007.
Laura E. Huggins	"Get Real on Going 'Green,'" *Washington Times*, April 18, 2008.
Kiki Namikas	"Boiling Point: The Campus Climate Movement Plays Political Hardball," *Earth Island Journal*, Winter 2008.
Rick Newman	"The Green Mirage," *U.S. News & World Report*, October 30, 2007.
Ted Nordhaus and Michael Shellenberger	"Second Life: A Manifesto for a New Environmentalism," *New Republic*, September 24, 2007.
Mark Rice-Oxley	"Never Mind Altruism: 'Saving the Earth' Can Mean Big Bucks," *Christian Science Monitor*, October 25, 2006.
Kate Sheppard	"The Green Gap," *The American Prospect*, May 2008.
Jennifer Weeks	"Buying Green," *CQ Researcher*, February 29, 2008.

For Further Discussion

Chapter 1

1. In an interview with Decca Aitkenhead, James Lovelock claims that the damage done to the Earth will have devastating consequences. Jon Entine believes that such claims are alarmist. Despite quite different opinions on whether the Earth faces an environmental crisis, on what do both authors agree? Explain your answer, citing examples from the viewpoints.

2. William Chandler contends that global warming is caused by human activities and therefore requires solutions that limit these activities. Dennis Behreandt disputes Chandler's claim, arguing instead that global warming is more likely a natural phenomenon. Identify the evidence that each author uses to support his claim. Which evidence do you find more persuasive? Citing from the viewpoints, explain.

3. Gedden Cascadia believes that overpopulation poses a serious environmental threat. Ross B. Emmett disputes this claim. Both authors have quite different views on human nature. Identify these differing views, citing from the viewpoints. With which view of human nature do you agree? Explain your answer.

4. Of the threats to the environment explored in this chapter, which do you think is the most serious? Explain, citing from the viewpoints.

Chapter 2

1. Sven Teske, Arthouros Zervos, and Oliver Schäfer claim that renewable energy is cheaper and better for the environment. Lyndon Thompson and Rory J. Clarke make the

opposite claim, arguing that renewable energy is more expensive and has its own negative impact on the environment. The authors on both sides of this question cite evidence to support their claims. Citing the evidence, which viewpoint do you find more persuasive?

2. The Union of Concerned Scientists and analysts Peter Schwartz and Spencer Reise agree that nuclear power is a proven and clean source of energy. They disagree, however, concerning its safety and its impact on the environment. How do the affiliations of the authors of these viewpoints influence their arguments? Does this influence make their arguments more or less persuasive? Citing from the viewpoints, explain your answer.

3. Fred Pearce disputes Environmental Defense's claim that emissions trading will motivate businesses to reduce the greenhouse gas emissions that lead to global warming. Pearce argues that energy efficient businesses will not work to become more efficient; they will simply trade their credits to businesses that are inefficient. Citing from the viewpoints, explain which argument do you find more persuasive.

4. Of the policies to reduce global warming explored in this chapter, which do you think will be most effective? Explain, citing from the viewpoints.

Chapter 3

1. Kate Soper believes that Western consumerism threatens the environment. Paul Wapner and John Willoughby do not dispute this claim, but suggest that efforts to reduce individual consumption simply deplete other resources. Both viewpoints argue for fundamental changes to address environmental challenges. What are these changes and which do you think are more likely to reduce the impact of the Western lifestyle on the environment? Explain, citing from the viewpoints.

2. Ellen Ruppell Shell and Dana Joel Gattuso disagree concerning the impact of electronic waste on the environment. These authors use very different rhetorical techniques to support their positions on this issue. Identify the rhetorical techniques used in each viewpoint, and explain which strategy you find more persuasive. Citing from the viewpoints, explain your answer.

Chapter 4

1. Carl Pope and Thomas A. Moser disagree about the impact of environmental activism. How do the affiliations of the authors influence their arguments? Does this influence make their arguments more or less persuasive? Explain, citing from the viewpoints.

2. In an interview with Jenny Shank, Josh Dorfman argues that because people will continue to consume, buying green is one way to improve the environment. Monica Hesse claims that this solution is inadequate. Dorfman and Hesse have a different definition of what it means to be green. Which definition do you believe should be used when discussing environmental policies? Explain your answer.

3. Of the policies to reduce global warming explored in this chapter, which do you think will be most effective? Explain, citing from the viewpoints.

Organizations to Contact

The editors have compiled the following list of organizations concerned with the issues debated in this book. The descriptions are derived from materials provided by the organizations. All have publications or information available for interested readers. The list was compiled on the date of publication of the present volume; the information provided here may change. Readers need to remember that many organizations take several weeks or longer to respond to inquiries.

American Council on Science and Health (ACSH)
1995 Broadway, 2nd Floor, New York, NY   10023-5860
(212) 362-7044 • fax: (212) 362-4919
e-mail: acsh@acsh.org
Web site: www.acsh.org

ACSH is a consumer education consortium concerned with environmental and health-related issues. The council publishes the quarterly periodical *Priorities*, position papers such as "Global Climate Change and Human Health," and numerous reports, including *Regulating Mercury Emissions from Power Plants: Will It Protect Our Health?* and *Scrutinizing Industry-Funded Science: The Crusade Against Conflicts of Interest*, which are available on its Web site.

Basel Action Network (BAN)
c/o Earth Economics, Seattle, WA   98104
206-652-5555 • fax: 206-652-5750
e-mail: inform@ban.org
Web site: www.ban.org

BAN's mission is to confront what it considers to be the global environmental injustice and economic inefficiency of trade in toxic wastes, products, and technologies. The organization promotes sustainable and just solutions to the consumption and disposition of waste, including the banning of the waste trade. It promotes green, toxic free, and the democratic design of consumer products. BAN's Web site provides access to e-waste news articles, reports, and speeches.

Bluewater Network
311 California Street, Suite 510, San Francisco, CA   94104
(415) 544-0790 • fax: (415) 544-0796
e-mail: bluewater@bluewaternetwork.org
Web site: www.bluewaternetwork.org

The Bluewater Network, which joined with Friends of the Earth in April 2005, works to stop environmental damage from vehicles and vessels, and to protect human health and the planet. It promotes policy changes in government and industry to reduce dependence on fossil fuels and to eradicate other root causes of air and water pollution, global warming, and habitat destruction. On its Web site the Bluewater Network publishes fact sheets, news, and articles on water-related environmental issues.

Canadian Centre for Pollution Prevention (C2P2)
215 Spadina Avenue, Suite 134, Toronto, Ontario   M5T 2C7
(800) 667-9790 • fax: 416-979-3936
e-mail: info@c2p2online.com
Web site: c2p2online.com

The Canadian Centre for Pollution Prevention is Canada's leading resource on ways to end pollution. It provides access to national and international information on pollution and prevention, online forums, and publications, including *The Citizen's Guide to Pollution Prevention* and the newsletter *at the source*, which C2P2 publishes three times a year.

Cato Institute
1000 Massachusetts Avenue NW
Washington, DC   20001-5403
(202) 842-0200 • fax: (202) 842-3490

e-mail: cato@cato.org
Web site: www.cato.org

The Cato Institute is a libertarian public policy research foundation that aims to limit the role of government and protect civil liberties. In addition to a wide range of journals and newsletters, Cato publishes books, including *Meltdown: The Predictable Distortion of Global Warming by Scientists, Politicians, and the Media*. Publications offered on its Web site include recent issues of the bimonthly *Cato Policy Report*, the quarterly journal *Regulation*, policy studies, and opinions and commentary.

Competitive Enterprise Institute (CEI)

1001 Connecticut Avenue NW, Suite 1250
Washington, DC   20036
(202) 331-1010 • fax: (202) 331-0640
e-mail: info@cei.org
Web site: www.cei.org

CEI is a nonprofit public policy organization dedicated to the principles of free enterprise and limited government. The institute believes private incentives and property rights, rather than government regulations, are the best way to protect the environment. CEI's publications include the bimonthly newsletter *CEI Planet*, the e-mail newsletter on environmental issues, *EnviroWire, On Point* policy briefs, and the books *Global Warming and Other Eco-Myths* and *The True State of the Planet*. Recent publications, including articles and editorials, such as "Greens Aim to Take Us Forward to the Past" and "The Real Population Bomb," are available on its Web site.

Earth Island Institute (EII)

300 Broadway, Suite 28, San Francisco, CA   94133-3312
(415) 788-3666 • fax: (415) 788-7324
Web site: www.earthisland.org

Founded in 1982 by veteran environmentalist David Brower, EII develops and supports projects that counteract threats to the biological and cultural diversity that sustain the environment. Through education and activism, EII promotes the conservation, preservation, and restoration of the Earth. It publishes the quarterly *Earth Island Journal*. Recent articles are available on the EII Web site, including "Mirage: Climate Change Threatens to Dry Up the Southwest's Future" and "Pink Water: Plastics, Pesticides, and Pills Are Contaminating Our Drinking Supply."

Environment Canada
351 St. Joseph Boulevard, Place Vincent Massey, 8th Floor
Gatineau   K1A 0H3
(819) 997-2800 • fax: 819-994-1412
e-mail: enviroinfo@ec.gc.ca
Web site: www.ec.gc.ca

Environment Canada is a department of the Canadian government. Its goal is the achievement of sustainable development in Canada through conservation and environmental protection. The department publishes reports, fact sheets, news, and speeches, many of which are available on its Web site.

Environmental Defense Fund
257 Park Avenue South, New York, NY   10010
(212) 505-2100
Web site: www.environmentaldefense.org

Founded by scientists in 1967, the Fund conducts original research and enlists outside experts to solve environmental problems. The advocacy group forms partnerships with corporations to promote environmentally friendly business practices. On its Web site, the Fund publishes news, fact sheets, reports, and articles, including the brochure, "Cap and Trade 101" and the report *Offsets: Reducing Global Warming Pollution Quickly and Affordably*.

Environmental Justice Resource Center (EJRC)
223 James P. Brawley Drive, Atlanta, GA   30314
(404) 880-6911 • fax: (404) 880-6909

e-mail: ejr@cau.edu
Web site: www.ejrc.cau.edu

Formed in 1994 at Clark Atlanta University, EJRC serves as a research, policy, and information clearinghouse on issues related to environmental justice, race and the environment, civil rights, locations of environmental hazardous industries, land use planning, transportation equity, and suburban sprawl. Center officials assist, support, train, and educate people of color with the goal of facilitating their inclusion into mainstream environmental decision making. On its Web site the Center provides access to a wide variety of resources, including reports, articles, and testimony.

Environmental Protection Agency (EPA)

Ariel Rios Building, 1200 Pennsylvania Avenue NW
Washington, DC   20460
(202) 272-0167
Web site: www.epa.gov

The EPA is the federal agency in charge of protecting the environment and controlling pollution. The agency works toward these goals by enacting and enforcing regulations, identifying and fining polluters, assisting businesses and local environmental agencies, and cleaning up polluted sites. The EPA publishes speeches, testimony, periodic reports and regional news on its Web site.

Friends of the Earth

1717 Massachusetts Avenue NW, Suite 600
Washington, DC   20036-2002
(877) 843-8687 • fax: (202) 783-0444
e-mail: foe@foe.org
Web site: www.foe.org

Friends of the Earth is a national advocacy organization dedicated to protecting the planet from environmental degradation; preserving biological, cultural, and ethnic diversity; and empowering citizens to have an influential voice in decisions affecting the quality of their environment. It publishes the quarterly *Friends of the Earth* newsmagazine, recent and archived issues of which are available on its Web site as are fact sheets, news, articles, and reports.

Global Warming International Center (GWIC)
PO Box 50303, Palo Alto, CA   94303-0303
(630) 910-1551 • fax: (630) 910-1561
Web site: www.globalwarming.net

GWIC is an international body that provides information on global warming science and policy to industries and governmental and nongovernmental organizations. The center sponsors research supporting the understanding of global warming and ways to reduce the problem. It publishes the quarterly journal, *World Resource Review.*

GrassRoots Recycling Network (GRRN)
4200 Park Boulevard, #290, Oakland, CA   94602
(510) 531-5523 • fax: (510) 531-5523
Web site: www.grrn.org

GRRN's mission is to eliminate the waste of natural and human resources. The network advocates corporate accountability and public policies that eliminate waste and build sustainable communities. The GRRN Web site includes fact sheets, reports, and articles, including "Composting and Organics: Recycling vs. Bioreactors" and "Beyond Recycling: The Zero Waste Solution."

Greenpeace USA
702 H Street NW, Washington, DC   20001
(800) 326-0959 • fax: (202) 462-4507
e-mail: info@wdc.greenpeace.org
Web site: www.greenpeaceusa.org

Greenpeace opposes nuclear energy and the use of toxic chemicals and it supports ocean and wildlife preservation. It uses controversial direct-action techniques and strives for media coverage of its actions in an effort to educate the public. It publishes the quarterly magazine *Greenpeace* and the books *Coastline* and *The Greenpeace Book on Antarctica*. On its Web site Greenpeace publishes fact sheets and reports, including *Pushed to the Brink: The Oceans and Climate Change* and *Nuclear Power—Undermining Action on Climate Change*.

Heritage Foundation

214 Massachusetts Avenue NE, Washington, DC   20002-4999
(800) 544-4843 • fax: (202) 544-6979
e-mail: pubs@heritage.org
Web site: www.heritage.org

The Heritage Foundation is a conservative think tank that supports free enterprise and limited government. Its researchers criticize EPA overregulation and believe that recycling is an ineffective method of dealing with waste. Its publications, such as the quarterly *Policy Review*, include studies on the uncertainty of global warming and the greenhouse effect. The articles "CO2-Emission Cuts: The Economic Costs of the EPA's ANPR Regulations" and "Time to Fast-track New Nuclear Reactors" are available on its Web site.

Natural Resources Defense Council (NRDC)

40 W 20th Street, New York, NY   10011
(212) 727-2700
e-mail: proinfo@nrdc.org
Web site: www.nrdc.org

NRDC is a nonprofit organization dedicated to using both law and science to protect the planet's wildlife and wild places and to ensure a safe and healthy environment for all living things. NRDC publishes the quarterly magazine *OnEarth* and the bimonthly bulletin *Nature's Voice*. On its Web site NRDC provides links to specific environmental topics and news, articles, and reports, including *The Cost of Climate Change* and *Keeping Oceans Wild*.

Pew Center on Global Climate Change
2101 Wilson Boulevard, Suite 550, Arlington, VA   22201
(703) 516-4146 • fax: (703) 841-1422
Web site: www.pewclimate.org

The Pew Center is a nonpartisan organization dedicated to educating the public and policy makers about the causes and potential consequences of global climate change and informing them of ways to reduce the emissions of greenhouse gases. Its reports include *Designing a Climate-Friendly Energy Policy* and *The Science of Climate Change.*

Property and Environment Research Center (PERC)
2048 Analysis Drive, Suite A, Bozeman, MT   59718
(406) 587-9591
e-mail: perc@perc.org
Web site: www.perc.org

PERC is a nonprofit research and educational organization that seeks market-oriented solutions to environmental problems. The center holds a variety of conferences and provides educational material. It publishes the quarterly newsletter *PERC Reports*, commentaries, research studies, and policy papers. Various publications, including "Growing Green in Brown China," "Many Private Landowners Nurture Public Wildlife," and "Meet the Enviropreneurs of 2008," are available on PERC's Web site.

Resources for the Future (RFF)
1616 P Street NW, Washington, DC   20036
(202) 328-5000
Web site: www.rff.org

Founded in 1952, RFF is a think tank that pioneered the application of economics as a tool to develop effective environmental policy. It conducts independent research on global warming and other environmental issues. RFF publishes books and reports that present a broad range of approaches to the study of natural resources and the environment, including

Perspectives on Sustainable Resources in America and *From the Corn Belt to the Gulf: Societal and Environmental Implications of Alternative Agricultural Futures.*

Sierra Club

85 Second Street, 2nd Floor, San Francisco, CA   94105-3441
(415) 977-5500 • fax: (415) 977-5799
e-mail: information@sierraclub.org
Web site: www.sierraclub.org

The Sierra Club is a grassroots organization with chapters in every state that promote the protection and conservation of natural resources. The organization maintains separate committees on air quality, global environment, and solid waste, among other environmental concerns, to help achieve its goals. It publishes books, fact sheets, the bimonthly magazine *Sierra*, and the *Planet* newsletter.

Union of Concerned Scientists (UCS)

2 Brattle Square, Cambridge, MA   02238
(617) 547-5552 • fax: (617) 864-9405
e-mail: ucs@ucsusa.org
Web site: www.ucsusa.org

UCS aims to advance responsible public policy in areas where science and technology play important roles. Its programs emphasize transportation reform, arms control, safe and renewable energy technologies, and sustainable agriculture. UCS publications include the twice yearly magazine *Catalyst*, the quarterly newsletter *earthwise*, the electronic newsletter *Greentips*, and the reports *Walking a Nuclear Tightrope* and *Greenhouse Crisis: The American Response.*

Worldwatch Institute

1776 Massachusetts Avenue NW
Washington, DC   20036-1904
(202) 452-1999 • fax: (202) 296-7365
e-mail: worldwatch@worldwatch.org
Web site: www.worldwatch.org

The Worldwatch Institute is a nonprofit public policy research organization dedicated to informing the public and policy-makers about emerging global problems and trends and the complex links between the environment and the world economy. Its publications include *Vital Signs*, issued every year, the bimonthly magazine *World Watch*, the Environmental Alert series, and numerous policy papers and reports, including *Working for People and the Environment* and *Oceans in Peril: Protecting Marine Biodiversity*.

Bibliography of Books

David Archer   *Global Warming: Understand the*
                          Forecast. Malden, MA: Blackwell,
                          2007.

Allen Carlson and   *Nature, Aesthetics, and*
Sheila Lintott,   *Environmentalism: From Beauty to*
eds.   *Duty.* New York: Columbia University
                          Press, 2008.

Matthew James   *Fatal Misconception: The Struggle to*
Connelly   *Control World Population.* Cambridge,
                          MA: Belknap Press, 2008.

David Howard   *Ignoring the Apocalypse: Why*
Davis   *Planning to Prevent Environmental*
                          Catastrophe Goes Astray. Westport,
                          CT: Praeger, 2007.

Walter Kennedy   *Humanity's Footprint: Momentum,*
Dodds   *Impact, and Our Global Environment.*
                          New York: Columbia University
                          Press, 2008.

Daniel Faber   *Capitalizing on Environmental*
                          Injustice: The Polluter-Industrial
                          Complex in the Age of Globalization.
                          Lanham, MD: Rowman & Littlefield,
                          2008.

Elizabeth   *High Tech Trash: Digital Devices,*
Grossman   *Hidden Toxics, and Human Health.*
                          Washington, DC: Island Press, 2006.

Bernd
Hansjügens, ed.

Emissions Trading for Climate Policy: U.S. and European Perspectives. New York: Cambridge University Press, 2005.

Nathaniel O. Keohane and Sheila M. Olmstead

Markets and the Environment. Washington, DC: Island Press, 2007.

Eric Lambin

The Middle Path: Avoiding Environmental Catastrophe. Chicago, IL: University of Chicago Press, 2007.

Thomas E. Lovejoy and Lee Hannah, eds.

Climate Change and Biodiversity. New Haven, CT: Yale University Press, 2005.

Thomas P. Lyon and John W. Maxwell

Corporate Environmentalism and Public Policy. New York: Cambridge University Press, 2004.

Karl Mallon, ed.

Renewable Energy Policy and Politics: A Handbook for Decision-Making. Sterling, VA: Earthscan, 2006.

Robert Nadeau

The Environmental Endgame: Mainstream Economics, Ecological Disaster, and Human Survival. New Brunswick, NJ: Rutgers University Press, 2006.

William Nordhaus

A Question of Balance: Weighing the Options on Global Warming Policies. New Haven, CT: Yale University Press, 2008.

David Naguib Pellow

Resisting Global Toxics: Transnational Movements for Environmental Justice. Cambridge, MA: MIT Press, 2007.

Elizabeth Royte

Garbage Land: On the Secret Trail of Trash. Boston: Little, Brown, 2005.

Ronald Sandler and Phaedra C. Pezzullo, eds.

Environmental Justice and Environmentalism: The Social Justice Challenge to the Environmental Movement. Cambridge, MA: MIT Press, 2007.

Jerry Silver

Global Warming and Climate Change Demystified. New York: McGraw-Hill, 2008.

S. Fred Singer and Dennis T. Avery

Unstoppable Global Warming: Every 1,500 Years. Lanham, MD: Rowman & Littlefield, 2008.

Galen J. Suppes and Truman S. Storvick, eds.

Sustainable Nuclear Power. Boston: Elsevier/Academic Press, 2007.

Thomas H. Tietenberg

Emissions Trading: Principles and Practice. Washington, DC: Resources for the Future, 2006.

Ted Trainer

Renewable Energy Cannot Sustain a Consumer Society. London: Springer, 2007.

David G. Victor

Climate Change: Debating America's Policy Options. New York: Council on Foreign Relations Press, 2004.

Robert G. Watts — *Global Warming and the Future of the Earth*. San Rafael, CA: Morgan & Claypool, 2007.

Spencer Weart — *The Discovery of Global Warming*. Boston: Harvard University Press, 2004.

Roland Wengenmayr and Thomas Bührke, eds. — *Renewable Energy: Sustainable Energy Concepts for the Future*. Weinheim, Germany: Wiley-VCH, 2008.

Edward O. Wilson — *The Creation, An Appeal to Save Life on Earth*. New York: W.W. Norton, 2006.

Ernesto Zedillo — *Global Warming: Looking Beyond Kyoto*. Washington, DC: Brookings Institution Press, 2007.

David Zeigler — *Understanding Biodiversity*. Westport, CT: Praeger, 2007.

Index